PROJECT MANAGEMENT
SCHOLIA

PROJECT MANAGEMENT SCHOLIA

RECOGNIZING AND AVOIDING
PROJECT MANAGEMENT'S BIGGEST MISTAKES

GEORGE TILLMANN

Stockbridge Press

Project Management Scholia:
Recognizing And Avoiding Project Management's
Biggest Mistakes

Copyright © 2019 George Tillmann
All rights reserved.

Published by Stockbridge Press

For Ralph

He who has a brother has more than riches can buy.
~ African proverb

CONTENTS

CONTENTS (cont'd)

Preface

The common knowledge of a profession often goes unrecorded
in technical literature for two reasons:
one need not preach commonplaces to the initiated, and one should not attempt
to inform the uninitiated in publications they do not read.
~ Stephen Jay Gould

Fools you are...who say you like to learn from your mistakes...
I prefer to learn from the mistakes of others, and avoid the cost of my own.
~ Otto von Bismarck

Project Management Scholia? What are scholia?

Scholia are comments in the margins of books. They go back to scribblings in ancient Greek texts, but we are most familiar with them from writings of the Middle Ages. As monks copied books by hand, they would sometimes raise questions or provide comments in the margins of the text. Generations of monks would edit, improve, and expand those comments until they were either incorporated into the original work or became a book in their own right.

This book is such a work. If you are a project manager or desire to someday be a project manager, then your bookshelf should brim with the works of some of the greats in project management scholarship such as Yourdon, DeMarco, and Jones. This is not one of those books, but rather a collection of the scribblings you, or someone else, might have written or found in the margins of those books; or notes recorded from project team meetings; or feedback from interviews with users, business managers, or IT management about a project; or the talk heard around the table in the team breakroom; or any other place where the practical knowledge of project management is passed on. The aspirant can learn about new systems development and project management tools and techniques as well as which work, which do not work, and which to avoid at all costs.

The topics on the following pages are the often painful lessons learned, not from the library or the classroom, but from the corporate trenches of real-world systems development. These are not the civilized conversations debated with your college professor over high tea, but from the real-world slugfest in the mud, and the blood, and the beer.

Project management is a juggling act worthy of any circus. The successful project manager is a technician, politician, counselor, diplomat, enforcer, conjurer, administrator, bureaucrat, entrepreneur, entertainer, hit man, and, too often, zookeeper. Very few jobs require so many skills to be successful. Unfortunately, all too many project managers aren't successful. As many researchers have pointed out, project success is elusive with less than half of systems development efforts completing their original mission. Is the project manager the main problem? Probably not. However, if the string section sounds like a strangled cat, it is the orchestra leader who takes the heat. The same is true in project management. A vendor fails to deliver hardware on time, no office space for the team to work together in one place, staff with obligations outside the project—all of these are catalysts for failure, and the solutions to all eventually rest on the shoulders of the project manager.

Is this a piece of what the academics call, "original work?" Absolutely not. Pride is taken in having borrowed or stolen everything here. The first lesson any project manager novitiate should learn is, don't do anything original if you can avoid it. Other brave souls have gone before you and tried all of those silly things some coworker, classmate, or vendor convinced them to try. You now get to stand tall on the rubble of their careers, if, and only if, you are smart enough to learn from their mistakes.

The information contained here was gleaned from the memories, and sometimes nightmares, of project managers recounting the things they wished they knew and followed at some earlier time in their project management careers. If you spend any time in the old project managers home, you will hear a litany of, "If I only knew then what I know now." This book recounts sometimes exciting, sometimes disappointing, life-enlightening episodes gathered from personal history and from talking with dozens of experienced project managers who have either observed or lived through each of these mistakes.

Not every project manager agrees with every entry in this book. There are diverse opinions on which are significant problems and which are so obvious that they cannot see how anyone could make that mistake. However, all of the entries in this book are deemed worthy of discussion by multiple battle-hardened project managers.

So, to complement all those great tomes on project management adorning your bookshelf, this is a humble and unpretentious book that you can hide in a drawer that might just save your job.

By the way, it would be poetic justice, not to mention highly appropriate if you scribble a few notes in the margins of this book providing comments or even correcting what you believe are author mistakes.

The book is organized into five parts and eighteen chapters.

PART ONE: BEFORE PROJECT KICKOFF

Chapter 1 Not Defining Your Terms. IT and the user, or IT and a contractor, at loggerheads because of a contractual dispute? More than likely the problem is definitional. The chapter discusses the systems development problems that can arise owing to incomplete, inaccurate, or improperly used definitions. Not an overly exciting chapter but needed to get the most out of the remainder of the book.

Chapter 2 Confusing the *What* With the *How*. One of the biggest and most damaging mistakes systems developers make is wading into *how* the application should work before understanding *what* the user wants.

Chapter 3 Too Many News. IT wants and needs all that new stuff—hardware, networks, systems software, systems development tools, etc.—but it also needs a user mega-project to pay for them. However, mixing all that new stuff with a large business-critical application can spell disaster.

Chapter 4 The Big Bang Bust. Traditionally, large projects have a low success rate, while small projects have a higher success rate. This chapter deals with how to make that large project a small project.

Chapter 5 Planning for the Perfect. Project planning—specifically project estimating—is the single biggest sinkhole in systems development. This chapter deals with how to survive the entire forecasting fiasco with a semblance of your career intact.

PART TWO: GETTING THE PROJECT STARTED

Chapter 6 Screwing Up Staffing. Researcher after researcher has pointed out that the number one variable in project success is staff. This is a significant finding that IT works hard to ignore.

Chapter 7 The Fungible Fallacy. There are a few techniques and tips that makes project planning easier. This one is a double-edged sword.

Chapter 8 No Project Champion. Want your project to succeed? Don't say yes if you don't have a project champion.

Chapter 9 Not Taking Advantage of the Honeymoon Period. In the mire of managing user expectation, there are a few gifts. Unfortunately, few project managers take advantage of this one.

PART THREE: MID-PROJECT

Chapter 10 Slippage. It's bad enough when some project activity takes longer or costs more than planned. It's worse if you don't know how to account for it.

Chapter 11 Scope Creep. The slippery slope can wind up a sheer cliff if you are not careful. Here is some help.

Chapter 12 Not Reading the Danger Signs. Project managers are not Wile E. Coyote. If they don't see the cliff before going over it, it's too late. This chapter includes a few cliff-sighting tips.

Chapter 13 What Do You Mean by Communicate? You know those executives who pay all the bills? They want to hear what is going on in a way they understand.

Chapter 14 Not Recognizing That Half of Managing is Selling. You're a project manager and don't want to be a salesperson. Surprise, you are. Here's what to do about it.

PART FOUR: ENDGAME

Chapter 15 Failing Testing by Passing on Testing. "We can get back on schedule if we just...," famous last words.

Chapter 16 The Problem of Not Having Throwaway Code. This chapter tells you how to create gems that you then throwaway—or maybe not.

Chapter 17 No Post-Project Review. Survived the project? Want to make the next one easier?

PART FIVE: GILDING THE LILY

Chapter 18 And Now for Something Completely Different. A non-negative chapter with some rather positive advice from team room survivors.

George Tillmann
george_tillmann@gmx.com
georgetillmann@optonline.net

PART ONE

BEFORE PROJECT KICKOFF

Chapter 1

Not Defining Your Terms
or
Defining the Ill-Defined

The shepherd drives the wolf from the sheep's throat, for which the sheep thanks the shepherd as his liberator, while the wolf denounces him for the same act as the destroyer of liberty. Plainly, the sheep and the wolf are not agreed upon a definition of liberty.
~Abraham Lincoln

In 1998, NASA launched the Mars Climate Orbiter, a \$300+ million spacecraft that traveled more than 400 million miles to the red planet. Even with speeds exceeding 3 miles per second, the journey took almost 9.5 months. Upon reaching its destination, the spacecraft fired its rockets to ease into a Mars orbit. Radio transmission was disrupted as the craft spun behind the planet and was expected to only resume 21 minutes later as it reappeared on the other side. Only it didn't. The spacecraft was never heard from again.

NASA investigators determined that a *definitional problem* doomed the craft. The engine burn was timed to slow the craft down and place it in a safe orbit 68 miles above the surface of the planet. However, the instructions for the burn were wrong, resulting in the craft attempting to orbit Mars at a disastrous altitude of only 35 miles. The problem: The NASA's spacecraft was programmed to use the metric system while the commercial contractor sent burn information to NASA using the English system (pound-seconds instead of Newton-seconds). The burn lasted too long, the probe attempted too low an orbit, and burned up in the Mars atmosphere.

This is a pretty dramatic case of the definitional problem. The engineers' thinking was sound, their math was accurate, their numbers were correct, just the definition of those numbers (English versus metric) was misunderstood.

Information technology has its own definitional problems. Take 100 K. Is it 100 K bytes or 100 K bits? Programmers, who routinely deal with bytes, will assume that it's 100 K bytes. Network engineers, who routinely deal with bits, will naturally assume that its 100 K bits. Who is right?

A contentious area, fueled by definitional problems, is downtime. Imagine a situation where every Sunday at 2:00 a.m., IT takes email offline for preventive maintenance. At 2:10 a.m., the VP of Marketing tries to send an email to the head of Europe only to get a message that email is not available. Later that month, the VP of Marketing is surprised to see an IT report saying that there was no email downtime for that month. Result: The VP of Marketing resolves never to trust IT reports again.

Who is right? Was email down that month? Depends on what your mean by *down*. IT believes that *down* means an unscheduled interruption in service, while the user believes that *down* means the service is unavailable, regardless of cause. Both groups have well formulated, complete, and appropriate definitions, both definitions are adequate, accurate, and acceptable, they just don't agree.

Of more consequence is user management being told by IT that the total cost of their new accounting system will be $1,000,000, only to find that IT did not include in its budget transition, end-user documentation, or training costs. Question: who is correct? Answer: both.

When multiple parties are right, or at least not wrong, then the basis of the disagreement is probably definitional. In the example above, IT believes that the development cost consists of the hardware, software, and staffing expenses to analyze, design, code, and test a system, but not implementation, user documentation, and user training charges, which are to be borne by the user organization. The user believes that the check he wrote for developing the system was the entire cost of getting his new application up and running, and is unaware of any additional "hidden" costs (think dealer preparation fee).

THE PROBLEM

Arguably, half of all IT-user disputes are definitionally based or exacerbated.

The *definitional problem* appears in multiple forms.

Multiple Well-Defined Definitions

One word or concept can have multiple legitimate and accepted but inconsistent definitions. Each party is using a formal definition that is well defined, correct, and broadly accepted by users in the field, just different.

The NASA case is a good example of this. Both the NASA team and the external contractor used complete, accurate, and accepted definitions of thrust. Each used its definition correctly and arrived at a situationally correct answer. Each team was aware that there were two distinct legitimate definitions. Unfortunately, each team assumed that the other team was using the same definition it was.

In like manner, temperature can be described using both the centigrade (Celsius) and Fahrenheit scales. Both are acceptable, well defined, and broadly used, but don't confuse them. Is 70 degrees comfortable? Well if it is Fahrenheit it is, but if the temperature is 70 degrees centigrade you will cook at what is 158 degrees Fahrenheit.

There are some interesting words in this category. Take *cleave*. It has two well defined, correct, and accepted definitions. One definition is to adhere closely or cling, as in a child cleaves to its mother. The second definition is to split, cut, or divide, as in a butcher cleaves the meat. Two legitimate definitions that have totally opposite meanings. Depending on which definition used, there could be a significantly different ending to the King Solomon story.

Multiple But Not All Well-Defined Definitions

One word or concept can have multiple definitions, with at least one a legitimate, detailed, and correct definition and at least one an inexact, although popular, definition.

This is a huge category that can be very frustrating for professionals. It usually involves a very technical and exact definition that is used by professionals in a field and the same word having a similar but much less exact definition used by non-professionals.

Take the word, *theory*. For a scientist a theory is a proposition that has been tested, probably multiple times, and has been proven to be sufficiently correct to predict future events. In empirical science there is no higher state of truth. The popular definition of theory is quite different. Non-scientists use the word theory to mean unproven and, at best, a guess.

The ambiguous use of theory has led to some interesting if fruitless discussions. Anti-evolutionists point out that evolution is only a theory and therefore not proven science. Scientists say that the fact that it's a scientific theory says that it is proven.

In IT, there is a similar problem, although with much less dire consequences. For technical people, K (as in 100 KB) represents 1,024 units. However, owing to the popularity of cell phones and laptops, K is also in the public domain, where even middle school kids can compare the memory size of their iPads. However, if you ask 100 people on the street what K stands for, probably more than 95 will say 1,000. Not 1,024.

Non-Specific, Fuzzy, or Incomplete Definitions

While there are words that do not have any specific and well accepted definitions, the majority of people know or "think" they know what they mean.

Many projects define effort in *person-hours*, *person-months*, or *person-years*; where person-year is the work one person routinely completes in one calendar year. Person-months (the successor to the socially insensitive man-month) are everywhere in IT and throughout many non-IT project-focused organizations as well. It is not an overly technical term and probably 95 percent of the people you meet on the street will tell you they know what it means. It is undoubtedly one of the most ubiquitous project-related terms. But what does it mean? Exactly how much work gets done in a person-year? Experience shows that the IT *year* can vary from fewer than 1,500 work hours to more than 2,000 hours. Why the difference? Many organizations remove activities such as vacation, training, and administrative time from the person-year. Other organizations believe that these activities are the *cost of doing business* and should be included in the definition. Some take a stand in the middle counting certain activities in the person-year, such as administrative time, but precluding others, such as vacations. Yet, anecdotal evidence indicates that fewer than one IT organization in four has an exact definition of effort, formally publishes the definition, communicates it to relevant parties, and ensures that whenever it is used it is used correctly.

Some similar definitional problems arise from concepts that range from vague to arcane. Take *lines of code (LOC)*, a concept used by many organizations, researchers, and authors, to define work required to build a system, or mathematically calculate work completed, or maintenance effort that will be required for completed systems. (COCOMO the project estimating method uses *lines of code* as its basic input.) Invariably questions arise. Are programmer comments included in LOC or not? Comments can account for half the carriage returns in a well-written program. What about a line versus a statement? Some programmers make each statement one line; other spread some statements over multiple lines; while a few cram multiple statements into a single line. Which is correct?

This problem can appear in IT where two project teams, or an IT organization and an external contractor, have different and poorly communicated definitions for common systems development words.

Obfuscation

Sometimes words are used to hide rather than elucidate meanings. Just bought a 2017 Ford Focus? That's a *used car*, while the 2016 BMW across the street is a *pre-owned vehicle*.

Interested in decision support systems (DSS)? Well that's old hat. Years ago the DSS gave way to executive information systems (EIS). The difference? Well, if there is any, then at least 90 percent of it is marketing hype. The EIS? Well it was replaced with online analytical processing (OLAP). The difference? You guessed it. OLAP? Well it was replaced by, er, was it business intelligence (BI) or predictive modeling (PM)? Whatever! Were all of these the same? No, there were differences and improvements. Did all deserve a different name? No. General Motors might change the design of the Corvette every year, but they still call it a Corvette.

The same is true for iterative-incremental development. Rapid application development (RAD), became prototyping, which became extreme programming, which became agile development, and a few others in between. Are they all the same? No. Are they very different? No. Do they deserve different names? Well, if you are selling one of them then, yes, otherwise…

Sometimes obfuscation is done for a good, though possibly misguided, reason. Take mental retardation—a terrible and tragic brain disorder that adversely affects intelligence. Not only is it a horrendous disease, but the terms describing it have been used pejoratively as an insult to hurt and mock others. Once legitimate medical terms, such as feebleminded, cretin, and retarded, were degraded over time into slurs and insults. As a result, the mental health establishment routinely changes terms to avoid unnecessary pain. Wikipedia calls this the "euphemism treadmill." You can almost identify the decade a report was written by knowing which terms were popular in medical journals. Today, feebleminded, cretin, and retarded have given way to *developmentally* or *intellectually disabled,* or *mentally challenged.* Time will tell whether these terms will eventually slip into misuse.

The downside of redefinition is the loss of communicative value. Parents sitting before a psychologist and being told that their child is *intellectually special* might not understand the severity of the situation. *Retarded* is certainly more emotionally charged than *intellectually special,* but it also might do a better job of communication.

Other than sparing people emotional trauma, there is little justification for *obfuscation.* Marketing might have made *obfuscation* an art, but IT is not far behind. Who else has the cojones to call a bug an "unintended feature."

WHAT YOU CAN DO

This is one of the few IT areas where the solution is relatively simple, easy to implement, and painless to use.

Define, Define, Define

It might take a little upfront effort, but all technical and even business terms should be formally defined and placed in a project glossary. Do it once and it can be used again and again. The project glossary can be an appendix to reports, a chapter in development documents, or referenced as a stand-alone text.

Definitionally challenged? Find a source (book, vendor documents, websites, etc.) that you can live with *in toto* or as input to your own project glossary.

Define First, Then Develop

The project glossary should exist before any development is started, planning completed, or costs discussed. This is important for two reasons.

First, it is easier to gain agreement on terms before anyone has a vested interest in the definition. Agreement on who will pay for end-user training or error correction before any contracts are signed is a lot easier than the argument that can occur after budget finalization. Down the road surprises are almost never good.

Second, a number of mid- or post-project disagreements can be settled easily by referring to published and agreed-upon definitions. The same is true within the project team. Defining documentation or testing can abrogate many potential project squabbles as team leaders maneuver to meet deadlines.

Agreement On *Operational Definitions* Is Required; Agreement On *Conceptual Definitions* Is Not

A *conceptual definition* is an intangible, theoretical, and abstract concept that you hold to be true. You might believe that life starts at conception, or that climate change is a hoax, or that existence is not a predicate. That is your right.

An *operational definition*, also called a *working definition*, is an agreement to use a precise definition in a specific context. The context for an operational definition can be temporary (for before 2000 or starting next year, etc.) or limited to a specific project, department, location, company, or even country. Operational definitions make it easier for everyone on a team to work together. For example, you might strongly disagree with the team's definition of temporary storage, but, for the purposes of communication and team harmony, you agree to use it during the project.

Keep the Definitions Updated

Technology changes rapidly and vendor marketing terms even more so. The project glossary should be revisited at the beginning of each project to see whether in any definitions need to be modified, new terms introduced, or old terms removed.

Will these four remedies really help? Let's take a look.

Multiple Well-Defined Definitions. One word or concept but multiple legitimate and accepted but inconsistent definitions.

- **Define, Define, Define.** There are many fine books as well as organizations such as the Project Management Institute that publish glossaries that any team can agree to use.

- **Define First, Then Develop.** Ensures that everyone on the team is using the same definitions right from get-go.

Multiple But Not All Well-Defined Definitions. One word or concept with multiple definitions, at least one legitimate, detailed, and correct definition and at least one that is an inexact although popular definition.

- **Define, Define, Define.** A reputable source will ensure that non-technical definitions are excluded.

Non-Specific, Fuzzy, or Incomplete Definitions. Words that do not have any specific and well-accepted definitions but the majority of people "think" they know what they mean.

- **Agreement On *Operational Definitions*.** If official definitions are not available, then the team can create working or temporary ones just for use during the project.

- **Define First, Then Develop.** The working or temporary definitions need to be defined and shared with the team before any work begins.

- **Keep the Definitions Updated.** Because the definitions are working or temporary, they might need to be modified or updated during the project.

Obfuscation. Sometimes words are used to hide rather than elucidate meanings.

- **Define, Define, Define.** A reputable source will ensure that there is little wiggle-room for those wishing to hide information.

- **Agreement On *Operational Definitions*.** If official definitions are not available, then the team can create working or temporary ones that avoid confusing language.

- **Define First, Then Develop.** Ensures that everyone is on the same project glossary page.

In Summary

IT, users, and management occasionally use concepts and words that are undefined, incorrectly defined, or incompletely defined, leading to sometimes serious misunderstandings. Compounding the problem, the various parties might not know that those they are trying to communicate with do not share their definitions. If a project manager wants to succeed, then everybody (team members, users, management, etc.) must understand, agree with, and use the same terms in the same way.

Unless you are a lexicographer, you probably do not find the subject of terminology that interesting and certainly not as a part of project management. It does have a sort of bowtie image. However, it is the first chapter in this book for one very important reason. All of the problem and solution areas in this book involve IT and sometimes even business terminology. It is important that readers understand what is being said, even if they do not necessarily agree with the definitions used.

THE TAKEAWAY

- Definitional problems (lack of definitional agreement, multiple definitions, incomplete definitions, and obfuscation) have caused IT considerable time, money, and user good will.

- Create a project glossary or designate an existing glossary as the project glossary before project kickoff to minimize confusion down the road.

- No good definitions? Then create working or temporary definitions—a, perhaps temporary, agreement on words and meanings used during development. Nothing fancy. You're not Daniel Webster.

Chapter 2

Confusing the *What* With the *How*
or
The *When*, *Why*, and *Where*
of Dealing With the *What* and *How*

It isn't that they can't see the solution. It's that they can't see the problem.
~ G. K. Chesterton

Imagine you are building a house. You get all your tools, lay out the lumber, and start constructing the first room. As you are building the room, you decide if it's a living room, or a kitchen, or a bathroom. When you finish the first room you start on the second, again deciding, as you build, what kind of room it will be.

Let's face it, no one would do that. A rational person would first figure out what the house should look like, the number of rooms it needs to contain, how the rooms are connected, etc. When the plans for the house are complete, then the correct amount of supplies can be delivered, the tools taken out, and construction begun. Architects work with paper and pen to plan the house, then, and only then, carpenters work with tools and lumber to build it. Everyone associated with home building knows that you plan first and then you construct.

If you learned anything new from the two previous paragraphs, then you should never go near an Ikea store. For the rest of us, the aforesaid two paragraphs are just good common sense...with one glaring exception. Some systems developers consistently confuse planning with building.

Arguably *the fundamental principle of systems development* (FPSD) is to figure out *what* the system is supposed to do before determining *how* to do it. *What* does the user want? *What* does the system have to do? *What* should system output look like? When the *what* is understood then the *how* can start. *How* will the system do it? *How* should the system generate needed output? *How* is how users get *what* they want.

Systems development methodologies are all based on FPSD *(the fundamental principle of systems development)*—figure out the *what* before the *how*. Don't start implementing, don't start coding, don't start designing—until you understand *what* the user wants.

THE PROBLEM

Placing the *how* before or in place of the *what* can result in some particularly prickly situations, such as leaving out or improperly implementing important functionality, requiring extensive rework, and trashing schedules and budgets.

Ensuring FPSD (the *what* before the *how)* is usually associated with two realities. The first is that everyone in systems development (not to mention the rest of the world) agrees FPSD is not only true, but obviously true. The second is that the first reality is routinely ignored in systems development.

Why? How could something so well understood be so ignored? Here are four common reasons.

Impatience—Excited to Get Started

Many in IT (the author included) started their career as programmers. Many future analysts, data architects, and project managers started out as coders. It is not surprising because much of the average college computer science or information technology curriculum is devoted to programming (design, coding, and testing). In addition, programming is a common entry-level position in many IT shops. It is understandable that many of the new (and not so new) project team members are anxious to start hacking (the original definition) away. In their haste FPSD is not so much ignored as short-changed—corners cut, important (sometimes annoying) users not interviewed, schedules compressed, etc. The result is an incomplete understanding of exactly *what* is wanted by users.

Not Understanding the Value of Analysis

Analysis, or whatever your call it (requirements, logical design, system definition, etc.) is the process of learning the *what* from the user, documenting what the analyst leaned, and then communicating it to those who will carry out system design (the *how).* However, analysis has endured some heavy criticism over the past few decades. Some feel that it is overly laborious, time consuming, error prone, or just not needed at all. The result can be an incomplete understanding of *what* the new system needs to do.

Part of the reason for inadequate analysis is the word itself. Analysis is used here as an activity to study the business to determine what the system has to do. However, the word is also closely associated with a phase of the waterfall system development life cycle (SDLC). For too many developers the question becomes, if the project will not be using the waterfall approach, then why perform analysis? Good question...which leads to the section below.

Rejection of Waterfall Approach

The waterfall SDLC is viewed by many as a relic of IT's past, offering little for today's developers. Unfortunately, the *what-how* distinction is closely tied to this approach (they came about around the same time), so any rejection of the waterfall approach contributes to skepticism regarding any *what-how* talk.

For those of you who just recently moved out of your cave, the waterfall SDLC consists of a series of sequential phases. Each phase is only executed once at the completion of the previous phase. A simple waterfall approach might consist of five phases: analysis, design, coding, testing, and installation (Figure 2.1). Analysis would be the phase in which *what* the user wants is understood, design defines the *how*, while coding constructs the programs to make the *how* real.

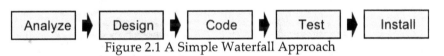

Figure 2.1 A Simple Waterfall Approach

In this approach, the analysis phase is completed before the design phase starts. The same is true for the other phases as well.

The waterfall approach has a number of problems, but two stand out. First is time. For a large project, each phase might take 6 months. It could be a year or more before the first line of the first program is written. In that time, user requirements might change multiple times, requiring a separate maintenance effort tied to the analysis and design phases just to keep system documents up to date.

Second, not everything in systems development is linear. There might be discoveries in design that require changes to analysis documents if not re-interviewing users. Coding problems could require design changes, and only God knows what testing will turn up. The do-it-once-and-forget-it nature of the waterfall approach is, in reality the *do-it–once-and-then-revisit-it-multiple-times-as-things-change* approach.

Starting eons ago (in IT time), developers adopted more flexible *iterative and/or incremental (I-I)* development approaches. Although there are dozens with various and cute names, they are all variations of the same theme: make systems development a series of small *iterative* steps each of which identifies a small portion of the overall *what* and an equally small portion of the *how*. In each step, create just a small *incremental* part of the system to see how well it works. Vendors like to depict I-I development as a spiral rather than a waterfall, showing the iterative and incremental nature of these approaches (Figure 2.2).

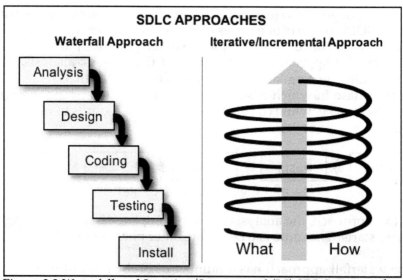

Figure 2.2 Waterfall and Iterative/Incremental (I-I) SDLC Approaches

Using an I-I approach such as prototyping, a session might consist of a developer sitting down with a user at a computer. The user tells the developer what is needed, and the developer codes a simple solution on the spot. The user can then react to the prototype, expanding and correcting it where necessary, until it is acceptable.

This is obviously a very different way to develop systems than the waterfall approach. What might not be so obvious is that the various I-I methodologies and techniques, such as rapid application development, prototyping, continuous improvement, joint application development, agile development, and so on, still involve figuring out *what* is wanted before determining *how* to do it.

Rather than looking at it as a picturesque spiral, an I-I approach can be viewed as a string (or vector for you programming buffs) of waterfall phases (Figure 2.3) where each cycle consists of a sequence of mini-analysis, mini-design, etc. phases. However, rather than each phase taking 6 months they could be no longer than 6 weeks, or 6 days, or 6 minutes.

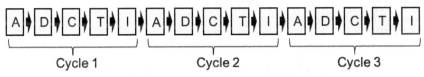

Cycle 1   Cycle 2   Cycle 3

Figure 2.3 Iterative/Incremental (I-I) Cycles

It might take a half-dozen cycles of sitting down with a user to figure out *what* is wanted and then coding the results (the *how*) before showing them to the user again for additional information or changes, but the principle is always the same—understand the *what* before determining the *how*.

However, too many developers throw out the baby with the bathwater. In rejecting the waterfall approach they mistakenly ignore the basic *what* before the *how*—the *fundamental principle of systems development*.

Bad Advice From Experts

Sometimes, believe it or not, the experts get it wrong. It happens.

Imagine a very data-driven systems development project that will use a relational database management system (RDBMS) as its core. Some systems developers, steeped in the science, traditions, and, let's face it, sophistry of their favorite model, believe that certain types of analysis are not needed if their model is used. For example, some relational model (the theory behind the RDBMS) advocates believe that users, such as business executives, can wade through foreign keys, normalization, and full functional dependency to define what their system should do without the need for IT help.

These misguided advocates cram physical design concepts (the *how*, such as junction tables and outer joins) into analysis interviews with users.

Misguided relational advocates are not the only abusers. Systems developers need to be wary of any vendor, method, technique, or tool that short-changes, ignores, misdirects, or undercuts a complete understanding of the *what*.

WHAT YOU CAN DO

What's a project manager to do? How do you ensure the *what* is understood before the *how*? There are two things the project manager can do—provide training and ensure discipline.

Training

The problem with most rules and regulations is that the reason they should be followed is not always obvious. Systems developers tend to be an independent and skeptical bunch. If it was easy to get them do to something, then documentation would be robust and project managers would earn half what they do now because their hardest job would have disappeared. No, managing a team of developers is like teaching an ethics class in Congress—difficult, underappreciated, and often exhausting. The one saving grace is that systems developers like to create great systems. The vast majority of analysts, designers and coders take great pride in doing a good job. The project manager needs to tap in to that enthusiasm.

The easiest way to get systems developers to do something (other than forbidding them from doing it) is to convince them that doing it is in their and the project's, interest and that separating the *what* from the *how* is in that category.

But wait. You can hear the challenge right now. "We are using agile development, so we don't need to separate the *what* from the *how*."

The answer is that the purpose of the *what-how* distinction is not to create a separate development phase but is to make developers *think before they act*—to ensure that before the design hits the page or a line of code entered on a screen, the problem is mulled over in those high-priced heads.

Tom DeMarco, in his book, *Controlling Software Projects,* introduces a simple experiment that perfectly demonstrates the value of thinking a problem through. It is ideal for a meeting of 15 developers or more, although it should work for a smaller group as well. Here is a slightly modified version of the experiment.

1. Activity 1: Ask the developers in the room to write the number "1" at the top of a piece of paper.

2. Tell them that when you say, "Go," they have seven seconds to write on that piece of paper the **total** amount of money, in paper and coins, on the person (pockets, pocketbook, socks, or wherever they keep money) of everyone in the room.

3. Quickly say, "Go."

4. Stop everyone after seven seconds and have them pass the pages to you.

5. Activity 2: Ask the developers to write the number "2" at the top of a second piece of paper.

6. Tell them that when you say, "Go," they have 30 seconds to write on the piece of paper the **total** amount of money, in paper and coins, on the person (pockets, pocketbook, socks, or wherever they keep money) of everyone in the room.

7. Quickly say, "Go."

8. Stop everyone after 30 seconds and have them pass the pages to you.

9. Activity 3: Ask the developers to write the number "3" at the top of a third piece of paper.

10 Tell them that when you say, "Go," they have 60 seconds to write on the page the actual amount of money, in paper and coins, they have on **their** own person.

11. Say, "Go."

12. Stop everyone after 60 seconds and have them pass the pages to you and then go on 10-minute coffee break.

13. Now you have some work to do. Average the monetary value on the pages labeled "1." Separately average the monetary value on the pages labeled "2." Total the monetary value on the pages labeled "3."

14. Present the results to the group. If you have done this right and the arithmetic gods are with you, the average monetary value of Activity 2 (the average of the amounts listed on the pages labeled 2) will be significantly closer to the total from Activity 3 (pages labeled 3) than the average monetary value of Activity 1 (the average of the amounts listed on the pages labeled 1.)

The results should show that taking just 23 seconds more to think through the problem resulted in a much more accurate result.

Separating the *what* from the *how* ensures that there is at least some "think time" between hearing what is wanted and creating it. The 23-second improvement shows that even when sitting down with a user in front of a workstation to build an iterative, incremental prototype, taking just a few seconds to fully understand *what* is wanted improves the result of *how* you do it. Imagine what you would get if the developer took a whole 5 minutes?

Is this approach counter to agile development or any iterative-incremental approach? No. Read the books and manuals more closely. There is not one author or vendor who does not believe that you should not think before you act. The problem is that many of them are not sufficiently vocal about the *value* of thinking before acting.

Discipline

As with anything associated with the project plan (See Chapter 5 Planning for the Perfect) the easiest way to get team members to do the right thing is to codify the behavior before the project kicks off. Rules, standards, and strong suggestions presented before a project starts are more likely to be accepted and followed by team members than mid-project changes, which can be seen as criticisms of team member behavior.

Whether its formal standards, classes, or just a project team meeting, the project manager needs to lay out the project rules of engagement, including such things as the method or approach used, communication protocols, putting the *what* before the *how*, time reporting, refilling the coffee pot, etc. This is the place to emphasize the importance of the *what* and the *how*, indicating that it is not just a best practice but also a project requirement.

Then comes the hardest part of the entire project—enforcement. The project manager needs to ensure that whatever rules of engagement were presented before kickoff (not just the *what* and the *how*) are followed. Failure to enforce the pre-project rules can undercut the project manager's credibility and authority. A few public executions early in the project do wonders for maintaining that project manager mystique.

In Summary

Note that the problem is not with the *how*—we have that one nailed down. The problem is with the *what*. Developers need to do a better job understanding *what* the user wants before jumping into the *how*. Some training might be called for—even requiring die-hard coders to take analysis (*what*) classes.

There is nothing new to buy—all the essentials are already in almost every method, technique, and tool. Developers just need to read the directions. Properly executed iterative and/or incremental approaches all have the developer understanding the *what* before the *how*, even if the wording is not as explicit as it should be. It's there, if not easily recognizable.

So the real answer to the *what* versus *how* conundrum is not some new fancy protocols, or programs, or steps to follow—just do the right thing.

THE TAKEAWAY

- The fundamental principle of systems development (FPSD) is to figure out *what* the system is supposed to do before determining *how* to do it.

- As important as FPSD is, it is often forgotten or ignored, particularly in the exhilaration of using some iterative-incremental (I-I) development approach.

- The solution is simple. It costs nothing and can be implemented right away. It just requires...
  — Training staff to take the time to really think through and understand the problem (the *what*) before committing to a solution (the *how*).
  — Discipline of the team members to follow the established principles and standards and the discipline of the project manager to enforce them.

Chapter 3

Too Many News
or
No News is Good News

There is nothing more difficult to take in hand,
more perilous to conduct, or more uncertain in its success,
than to take the lead in the introduction of a new order of things.
~ Niccolò Machiavelli

Imagine undergoing some serious surgery at your local hospital. As you are prepped for the operation, the nurse tells you that they are all excited about your surgery. It seems that the surgeon is very famous but also quite new to the hospital and the surgical staff has never worked with him before, and they are not familiar with the operating room procedures he requires. Further, there is exciting buzz about the new operating room technology that was delivered just the day before that will radically change how the operation is performed. You will be the first person they try it out on.

Farfetched? Of course it is. No one would ever put a new surgical team together with new technology and new operating room procedures with a real patient. It is a scenario for disaster. A new systems development project? Well, it's done all the time, isn't it!

THE PROBLEM

New IT technology is expensive whether it's hardware, software, tools (such as code generators, project management systems, or data-flow diagrammers), or techniques (such as data modeling, prototyping, or iterative development). Just purchasing one database management system can set an organization back six figures even before considering the cost of the required new hardware and staff training.

Many IT organizations cannot afford to purchase such items out of their operating budgets or even with the special budgets dedicated to small projects. Big-ticket items have to wait for the big systems development projects with their associated big budgets.

Beginning new, high-profile projects, with their funding coming from project sponsors outside IT, can be a time of renewal for IT organizations. That's the good news. The bad news is that all those new items increase the risk of project failure.

Go back to the surgery example. Being operated on by a famous surgeon is good. Having the latest operating technology is also a plus. Keeping hospital procedures up to date is a sign that the organization is trying to do better. Throwing them all together for the first time—not a good idea. Yet, that is exactly what IT does.

Let's turn the situation around and look at it from a different perspective. Assume that you are the project manager for a new, large, high profile, business critical application. Would you rather have—

- Skilled, experienced staff in systems development, who are knowledgeable about the business they will be supporting, or
  neophytes who are inexperienced, unskilled, and untested?

- Hardware, software, tools, and techniques the organization and staff have experience with, have successfully used before, are comfortable with, and are confident can do the job, or
  brand new items that are totally unknown and untested in your organization?

Yet, given two projects, one a 3-month, 9 person-month, internal to IT inventory system, and the other an 18-month, 200 person-month, business critical order processing system; which gets the tried and true tools and techniques, and which gets the high-risk, brand new, tools, and techniques? It's insane.

WHAT YOU CAN DO

OK, accepted, IT is adept at shooting itself in the foot. Ideally, you want your best-trained staff, using tried and true tools and techniques, on the most important projects, and you want to train staff and try, test, and learn how to use new tools and techniques on small, ideally internal-to-IT projects. How do you do that given that IT can only afford to purchase the new tools and techniques when undertaking a new business-sponsored project?

There are no great answers, but a few can provide some help. Look at the possible categories of projects.

Category 1: Small internal to IT project with little business-unit visibility. Ideal as the first project for new staff, hardware, software, networks, tools, or techniques.

Category 2: High-profile business-critical application with experienced project staff using tools and techniques staff are familiar with. The ideal situation.

Category 3: High-profile business-critical application with inexperienced staff or one new tool or technique the experienced project staff are not familiar with. Not ideal and with some risk, but with proper preparation, it is viable.

Category 4: High-profile business-critical application with inexperienced staff and one new tool or technique or experienced staff with two or more new tools or techniques. High risk of failure or seriously underperforming against expectations.

We will look at each in turn.

Category 1: Small Internal to IT Project—Little External Visibility

This is IT kindergarten or, to avoid bruised egos, IT boot camp. It is the ideal place to train new staff as well as try out new tools and techniques—even before you purchase them if you can talk the vendor into it. (Try asking. It sometimes works.) Experienced staff can use these projects as a safe harbor to learn new technology and hone new skills while newly promoted project managers can try out their newly acquired project management wings. Look at the aircraft industry rolling out a new plane. First flights are always short and close to the ground.

Some readers might think that Category 1 projects are "packing the house" with unnecessary work to train IT staff. Actually, the opposite is true. Forget the subject of this chapter for a minute and just look at IT. While IT is working to automate the business, it is often one of the least automated departments in the business. Certainly a case of the shoe maker's kids. Because of either priorities or budgets, IT is one of the most labor-intensive departments in many organizations with numerous opportunities for automation. However, getting approval for Category 1 projects can be a challenge.

Some strong IT management, a well prepared business case, and a good project champion (see Chapter 8 No Project Champion) should grease the skids for IT to identify, approve, and fund Category 1 projects, even if they are not kicked-off right away. Why not start them right away? Because the smart IT manager will always have a number of Category 1 projects waiting in the wings for just the right time (see below) to launch them.

Category 2: Business Critical-Experienced Staff-Existing Tools and Techniques

This category is IT's *raison d'être*—its reason for being. Low risk but high impact. Some would say that any high-profile business-critical application is high risk, but they are misusing the term risk. If the staff are experienced in the organization's tools and techniques, if they have built systems of similar size, and if they know the business, then the risk should be low. This does not mean that the impact of failure will be low. The risk of failure and the consequence of failure are two different things. Screw up a low-risk but high-profile project and you might be in a boat load of trouble. Drop the ball on a high-risk but low-profile project and you might escape unpleasant consequences.

Category 3: Business Critical-Inexperienced Staff or Experienced Staff with One New Tool or Technique

As pointed out above, many new tools and techniques have to wait for a big project to underwrite their cost. It's unfortunate but that is often the way things are. Inexperienced staff, or using a new systems development tool or technique, can significantly increase the risk of project failure, but there are a few things the project manager can do. A few options are below in order of preference.

Option A. Schedule a Category 1 project just before the Category 3 project

Because Category 1 projects are short and Category 3 project are long, it might be possible to schedule a Category 1 project, containing the new staff, tools, or techniques before the Category 3 project kicks off. A 2- to 3-month project might just provide the training and tool familiarity staff needs to get up to speed for that Category 3 project.

Option B. Run a Category 1 project simultaneously with the Category 2 project

Sometimes the Category 3 project needs to start immediately. In that case, IT might have to start the Category 1 project in parallel with the Category 3 project. Not ideal and the Category 1 project will probably negatively affect Category 3 schedules, but it is unavoidable. The more disparity between the Category 1 and Category 3 schedules (the longer the Category 3 project schedule) the better.

Option C. Build significant training and "prototyping" time into the Category 3 schedule

If running a Category 1 project before or in parallel with a Category 3 project is not possible, then the best the project manager can do is to build into the Category 3 project sufficient time to train staff on the new tools and techniques.

Note that Category 3 is defined as having just one new tool or technique or inexperienced staff. However, this rule is not hard and fast. If the new project development items are small or easy to use, or if they are used at different times in the project (such as during coding and testing), then the number of acceptable new items can be increased. However, the wise project manager must ensure that he or she is not fooling him/herself.

Category 4: Business Critical-Inexperienced Staff and One New Tool or Technique or Experienced Staff with Multiple New Tools or Techniques

Run! The risk of failure is very high. At the very least, this project will struggle with schedules and budgets as the staff works to get up to speed with the new development items it incorporates.

If you cannot escape this project, then your only hope is to try to turn the Category 4 project into a Category 3 project by bundling the time needed to learn to use the new technologies into the project schedules and budgets.

There is one potential saving grace for all but the most impossible projects. Staff

As is discussed in Chapter 6 Screwing Up Staffing, the most important factor in systems development is not the tools used, or the methods and standards of the organization, or the training available. The number one factor in project success is staff. A motivated, intelligent, and hardworking team can accomplish what all the tools and techniques in the world cannot. Oddly enough, as Chapter 6 Screwing Up Staffing points out, it is also the asset that IT and project managers are the least trained to acquire, develop, and keep.

THE TAKEAWAY

- IT faces a dilemma
  - — Investment in new systems development hardware, software, tools, and techniques often has to wait for new major business-critical systems development projects to pay for them.
  - — However, to minimize the risk of failure and undesirable business consequences, business-critical systems development projects deserve the most experienced staff, well trained in the use of tried and true development tools and techniques.

- The success of IT is determined by how well it resolves this dilemma.

- Prudent IT management will devise approaches that minimize the use of new tools and techniques while providing all possible training and experience for development staff by (in order of preference):
  - — Shifting, as much as possible, new staff, techniques, and tools to IT internal low-risk projects.
  - — Fronting business-critical projects using new staff, tools, and techniques with lower risk tasks and sub-projects.
  - — Any other means that allows staff to gain training and experience on new tools and techniques before applying them to high-risk tasks.

Chapter 4

The Big Bang Bust
or
Size Does Matter

Whenever something is wrong, something is too big.
~ Leopold Kohr

There is a potential train wreck out there. According to the trade press and peer-reviewed journals alike, systems development—the La Brea Tar Pit of IT—is in trouble. The much revered, and equally reviled, Standish Group's *Chaos Report* says that only about 30 percent of systems development projects succeed, 20 percent outright fail or are cancelled, and around 50 percent hobble along in some middle (between success and failure) state.

If you don't like the *Chaos Report*, there are a number of academic studies (hundreds of them) showing perhaps not as dire results but the same message—systems development is a blood sport.

THE PROBLEM

There is a fundamental flaw in how we build systems, and the project manager is caught in a real-life Catch-22 situation in trying to solve the problem.

Failed You Say?

It is interesting to note that while hundreds of academic papers and probably thousands of trade press articles bemoan the number of failed and underperforming projects; few, if any, objectively define "failed" or "under-performing." Instead these authors leave it to the systems developers or business users they interviewed or surveyed to express their opinion about project success.

Figure 4.1 is from a presentation("Understanding Technology Project Risks and Predicting Project Performance," by Andrew Gemino. http://slideplayer.com/slide/4551476/) on project risk covering more than 400 projects in the United States and the United Kingdom. The study shows that as the project headcount gets larger, the risk of underperformance gets higher. The larger the team size the greater the risk of failure. A 21 Full-time Equivalent (FTE) project is more than twice as likely to underperform as a 12-FTE project.

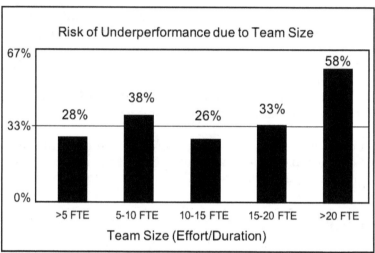

Figure 4.1 Risk of Underperformance Attributed to Team Size

OK, you want to reduce project risk, and the plan calls for too many people on the project. What do you do? Well, one option is to spread the project out over time thus requiring fewer staff. Figure 4.2 (from the same presentation) presents the level of risk based on the duration of the project. It shows that as the schedule extends out, the risk increases, with 20-month projects encountering twice the failure rate of 10-month projects. Reducing staff by extending the project duration introduces its own brand of risk. What's a project manager to do?

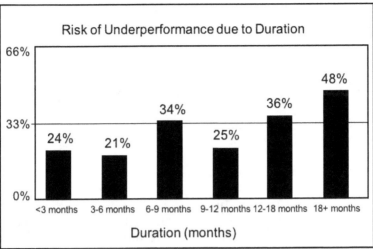

Figure 4.2 Risk of Underperformance Attributed to Duration

In fact, the project manager can't do much. As Figure 4.3 (same presentation) shows, it doesn't matter whether you thin the staff count and make the project longer or shorten the duration by adding staff, the devil is the project effort (person-months) required.

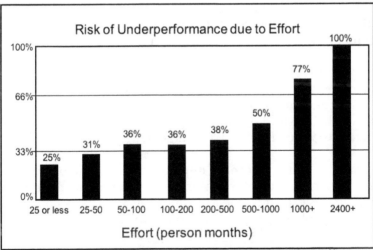

Figure 4.3 Risk of Underperformance Attributed to Effort

Thick or thin (many staff or few staff), long or short (long duration versus short duration), a 600 person-month project is twice as likely to underperform as a 20 person-month project. Put simply, Big is Bad.

WHAT YOU CAN DO

If big is bad, go small. Now, that should be the end of this chapter, but making big projects small is not so easy. Below are a few suggestions for accomplishing the *small is beautiful* effect.

Unum de Multis (Out of one, many—with apologies to the United States of America's motto)

The simplest way to reduce the risk of one big project is to make it multiple small projects. Slicing up the mega-project into bite-sized pieces is the best way of bringing in a large project. The result should be a number of subprojects, or phases, each with their own staff, project manager, goals, and deliverables. But exactly how big should the subprojects be?

Looking at the above bar charts one could conclude that a good team size would be in the range of fewer than 5 and up to 15 staff and a good duration somewhere in the 3- to 12-month range. Other authors have different but not terribly dissimilar numbers. Reviewing more than a dozen research studies, one would not be wrong in considering the average recommended team size seems to be in the four to seven range with a duration somewhere between 3 and 9 months. For simplicity, we will refer to the four to seven staff and 3 to 9-month duration as the *project sweet spot*.

The project sweet spot has a number of advantages. Its small headcount minimizes the required communication overhead (see Chapter 7 The Fungible Fallacy for a discussion of communication overhead), while the short duration mitigates the honeymoon problem (See Chapter 9 Not Taking Advantage of the Honeymoon Period).

The project sweet spot can be implemented serially or in parallel, or in any combination. A serial implementation has the mini-projects or phases executed one at a time, one after the other. If mega-project X is broken down serially into mini-projects A, B, and C, IT could theoretically use the same staff on each project. When A was completed, the team would move on to B, etc.

Parallel execution requires multiple project teams working on the different mini-projects at the same time. Parallel projects require different team members for each project—sharing staff across projects defeats the purpose of phasing.

Most phasing is serial because it is often the easiest way to divide a project, however, parallel phasing becomes more desirable when there are significant schedule pressures.

Phasing a project presents a number of challenges to IT and the project managers.

Technical Challenges to Project Phasing

Communication. One of the reasons to break up a large project into smaller pieces is the communication overhead problem—as the number of team members increases, the time and effort needed to keep everyone up to speed on project activity increases exponentially (see Chapter 7 The Fungible Fallacy). However, communication between teams is now needed, particularly if the phasing is parallel. While most intra-team communication is verbal, multi-team communication is often in writing, further increasing communication effort.

Partitioning. Exactly how to carve up the mega-project into multiple smaller pieces called mini-projects, subprojects, or phases is not always obvious. To do it right, the project manager (or whoever is tasked with parsing the project) needs a good understanding of the finished system and the tasks to build it.

Figure 4.4 shows a sample application data flow diagram (DFD). Processes or functions are depicted with rounded rectangles (example: A2, C1, etc.). Data stores or files (static data) are represented by open rectangles. Arrows depict the flow of data (data in motion) to and from data stores and communication (data sharing) between processes.

Selecting which processes to include in a mini-project is critical to development success. A phase or subproject should consist of processes where the communication (data sharing) between them is the highest. Phase boundaries should be defined to minimize cross-phase communication.

In Figure 4.4, processes A1, A2, A3, and A4 had the most significant communication between them and were kept together as a subproject, while a similar decision was made about processes B1, B2, and B3.

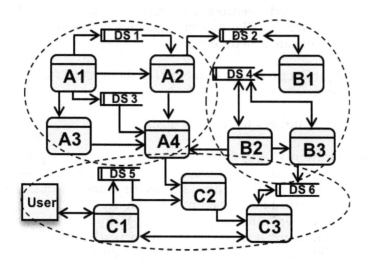

Figure 4.4 Megaproject Divided into
Three Subprojects (A, B, and C)

Budget. Partitioning a large project into bite-sized chunks can have a negative impact on effort and schedules. Communication overhead was discussed above, but in addition, multi-phased projects often require more analysis time (as business users are interviewed and re-interviewed) and testing time as the various sub-systems are integrated. Project managers for the various mini-projects need to incorporate the additional required effort and time into their individual plans.

Testing. The testing of the individual subprojects is usually neither harder nor easier then testing a similar portion of a mega-project, however, it can be different. If the mega-project was divided serially into phases, then testing other than in the first phase might require revisiting previous phases. For example, imagine a mega-project divided into subprojects A, B, and C. If the subprojects are executed serially, then testing subproject C might uncover changes needed to earlier completed subproject A. This problem is not limited to serially executed subprojects, but can also occur in parallel subproject development and even in a big bang approach where the work on the various portions of the system is completed at different times. However, it can be more prevalent and acute in serially developed subprojects.

Integration. A mega-project that is divided into components can require some effort to reintegrate once the mini-projects are complete. Not necessarily a difficult task, but one that needs to be taken into account.

Throwaway Code. Project phasing often requires additional non-application code that is not in the final production system. This code is required for the proper testing and integration of phase components that will eventually need to interact with components in other, not yet developed, phases (see Chapter 16 The Problem of Not Having Throwaway Code).

Management Challenges to Project Phasing

Slicing up what the user sees as a single project can present some management challenges.

User management. Senior business managers are often suspicious of any "project" that does not deliver the entire end result. They see a potential "bait and switch" where X was promised but they are only going to get X minus Y. Further, the additional time and dollars required for the phased system adds insult to injury. To top it off, they are skeptical of the argument that partitioning will eventually cost less (no write-offs for cancelled projects, or increased maintenance costs for underperforming systems) while increasing the odds of getting what they want.

IT management. Some IT organizations face a significant systems development backlog with needed applications having to wait months or even years before project work can begin. Some senior IT managers pressure current project managers to move ahead as quickly as possible to free up resources that can be applied elsewhere.

In spite of the cons, and because of the pros, phasing a large systems development project into manageable subprojects *is the single best planning action a project manager can take* to increase the odds of project success, and, in spite of the increased development costs and schedules, one of the cheapest.

THE TAKEAWAY

- Regardless of team size or duration, after a point, the greater the effort required (person-months) the greater the risk of project failure.

- Studies show that an ideal team size is between four and seven staff and 3 to 9-months duration—the so-called *project sweet spot*.

- Projects larger than the sweet spot should be broken up into smaller subprojects or phases, each with their own staff, project manager, goals, and deliverables.
  - The subprojects can be executed serially or in parallel depending on staff availability and schedule pressures.
  - Smaller subprojects reduce project risk but can involve integration costs (for example throwaway code) not in the original budget.

Chapter 5

Planning for the Perfect
or
When Perfect Turns Out to Be No Good

One does not plan and then try to make circumstances fit those plans.
One tries to make plans fit the circumstances.
~George Patton

Unless your systems development projects are limited to the classroom, before any real project work can begin, there typically needs to be a discussion of the effort—cost and time—it will take to deliver the system. In the real world, people who sign checks want to know what they are getting for their money and when they are getting it. This is also the beginning of one of the most significant and disruptive problems in systems development. Users don't want to buy a pig in a poke while developers don't want to commit to costs and schedules for an undefined project. Unfortunately, the buyer, the user in this case, has the stronger hand, while the seller, IT, has to compromise and give some estimates, although routinely accompanied by a long list of caveats frequently ignored by the user.

There is something else you need to know about estimating. Systems developers are terrible at it. Decades of research by hundreds of researchers shows that systems developers are awful at estimating the effort required to build a system. How bad?

According to a 2012 McKinsey-Oxford University study of 5,400 large-scale IT projects, 66 percent were over budget, 33 percent came in late, and 17 percent delivered less functionality than they promised (possibly because they were over budget or late).

Terminology

Before we start, let's have a short discussion of terminology. As with many expressions in IT, not everyone uses the same term in the same way or, equally confusing, they use different terms for the same concept (see Chapter 1 Not Defining Your Terms). The words used in this chapter might not always be the best but, for our purposes, they will do. However, because these definitions might vary from your organization's common usage, pay special attention to how they are used here.

Many systems developers use the terms *estimate* and *forecast* interchangeably. However, the two differ. An *estimate* is usually defined as an approximation of a calculable value. Some might say an educated guess. We estimate the number of beans in the "Guess the Number of Beans in the Jar" contest, or the amount of gas in the fuel tank, or the number of people who are coming for dinner. An estimate can be of something that happened in the past (how many beans were put in the jar), or the present (how much gas is in the fuel tank) or will happen in the future (how many people will be coming to dinner).

A *forecast* is a projection or prediction of a future event or state. Because no one can divine the future (even if they might be very sure of an outcome), all *forecasts* are also *estimates*. In systems development, you should *estimate* the number of lines of code in an existing application and *forecast* the number of lines of code in a future system. Although *forecast* is a subset of *estimate,* and project planning deals more with the future than the past, you would expect the term *forecast* would be used more than *estimate* but, unfortunately, this is not the case. Systems developers show a definite preference for *estimate* over *forecast*. Recognize that they are different, but expect them to be used interchangeably.

Effort is the amount of work needed or applied to complete some task. *Effort,* in systems development, is most commonly described in person-months, person-weeks, or person-days, where a person-month is the amount of work one person can produce in 1 month.

Cost refers to the funds (money for hardware, software, personnel, occupancy, etc.) required to complete the project.

Schedule, also referred to as *time,* is the calendar months (weeks, days, etc.) required to complete the project.

Functionality is what the system does or is supposed to do.

There are also a few bundled concepts, such as *budget* which usually consists of the *funds (costs)* and *time (schedule)* granted (allocated) to a project to complete its work. *Cost* and *time* are also linked with *functionality* to make up the *three planning variables,* so called because they are the three components of most concern by user management. Adding a bit of confusion to the mix, some people (users and IT) equate *budget* and *cost*, a *faux pas* we will try to avoid.

Actual refers to what really happened. Just as there are *cost, effort,* and *time estimates,* there are *cost, effort,* and *time actuals l.* If *effort* was *forecast* at 60 person-months but it took 75 person-months to complete the project, then the *actual effort* was 75 person-months.

The difference between *forecast* and *actual* is called *variance.* A *positive cost variance* occurs when less funds are expended than planned (*cost variance* equals *estimated (planned) cost* minus *actual cost*). A *negative variance* occurs when actuals exceed planned.

THE PROBLEM

While the bad news is that estimating is the most difficult part of project planning, the good news is a number of approaches, techniques, and tools can help the project manager tackle the problem. For decades, researchers have not only been lamenting IT forecasting incompetence, but they have also been busy developing approaches, techniques, and tools to make the job of estimating easier and the results more accurate.

A Sample of Estimating/Forecasting Approaches

The most popular estimating solutions center on history, formula, expert, and experimental based approaches. Below is a very quick look at these four popular approaches.

History-Based Estimating

History-based estimating approaches look into the organization's past and uncover the effort required for similar completed projects. If similar projects are not in the corporate history books, then algorithms and formulas, devised by practitioners and academics, can be applied to past work to extrapolate new project required effort. SLIM (Software Lifecycle Management), developed by Lawrence Putnam, is an example of a history-based technique.

SLIM analyzes past projects of all sizes and types to construct a mathematical model of the organization's individual development characteristics. The estimator enters into the model the lines of code that will be in the finished system, the historical productivity of the organization, and the time allocated to the project. A few formulas and the Putnam-developed scaling models generate an effort estimate in person–years to build the system.

The problem with history-based approaches is that they require good history. Unfortunately, many organizations do not have an honest and accurate picture of past development efforts. Why?

There are four major reasons for inaccurate project estimate history.

Changing user requirements. Users often change what the system needs to do. Mid-project changes can nullify original forecasts, yet the project plan is often only superficially modified, if at all, to accommodate the changes that endanger accurate end of project costs and schedules.

Function/task shedding by the development team. Fearing the wrath of IT or user management as a result of embarrassing (or career-threatening) overruns, some project teams secretly eliminate features or tasks to reduce required effort, hoping neither IT nor user management discover the subterfuge. Skipped end-of-year reports might not be noticed for many months, and users are almost never aware of short-changed testing or documentation tasks.

Inaccurate post-project documentation. Good history requires documenting particulars about a project, such as actual costs, staffing, and hours worked after its completion. The project actuals can then be compared with project estimates along with the reasons for any variance. However, few organizations have a formal post-project documentation period (see Chapter 17 No Post-Project Review), or if they do, the team, in its rush to move on to something else, cuts corners. The result is a sketchy picture of what actually happened during development.

Fudging. Project teams sometimes simply *cook the books* to make the numbers look better. Too many developers consider progress reporting a degrading form of self-incrimination.

All this means that the system envisioned on Day 1 of the project might not be the same system delivered on Completion-Day. Therefore, comparing Completion-Day actuals with Day 1 projections is often of limited value.

Formula-Based Estimating

Formula-based estimating approaches require the project manager to answer a number of questions that are then entered into a model. The model, a calculator- or computer-based program, then cranks out the effort needed. COCOMO (Constructive Cost Model) developed by Barry Boehm and Function Point Analysis, originally conceived by Allan Albrecht, are examples of formula-based techniques.

Boehm's COCOMO model is also history based, but the difference from Putnam's approach is that Boehm did the history work for you. Boehm studied a number of projects, and his analysis led to a series of formulas that model project effort. The project manager simple tells COCOMO the number of *lines of code* that will be in the desired system, and the effort to build it pops out.

Function point analysis is similar to COCOMO, but instead of lines of code inserted into a model, it uses business or end-user functions. The project manager counts the number of inquiries, inputs, outputs, internal files, and external interfaces in the intended system. Complexity is assessed for each function, and a number of points assigned. A simple display of information might require only one function point while a complex calculation might require 10. The points are summed, and that number is used to calculate development effort. For example, assuming a project size of 500 function points and a developer can complete 20 function points in 1 month, then the system would require 25 person-months of effort.

Most formula-based approaches require some project work before any estimates are available. Calculating lines of code or function points can require person-months of work before a useable estimate for the entire project is possible. This *pre-project project,* and its associated costs and schedules can stress organizations when the paying user wants a cost or time commitment before funding any exploratory work.

Expert-Based Estimating

Expert- or guru-based estimating approaches gather systems development and business experts together and, in an IT version of a séance, divine the effort required. The Delphi method is an example of a guru-based technique.

Expert-based estimating approaches require individuals with both project management and subject expertise, a rare commodity in many organizations. The experts are individually interviewed and/or complete surveys overseen by a facilitator. After the first round is complete all are shown the results, although they usually do not know who created which estimate. After the first round results are shared, there is a second or even a third round. Sometimes the last round is done as a group. The result is a group best educated guess of the effort required to complete the project. Unfortunately, even though their output is a well thought out educated guess, it is still a guess.

One challenge with the Delphi method is the quality and applicability of the questions, either asked in interviews or in the questionnaires the experts fill out. If the experts are asked the wrong questions or important questions are never asked, then the usefulness and value of the answers are problematic.

There is also a guru-based estimating approach cost issue. Identifying and scheduling the right experts, developing intelligent interview guides and surveys, conducting the sessions, and tabulating results takes time. A well run estimating task can easily take a calendar month and many person-months, once again raising the question of who will pay for it.

Experimental-Based Estimating

Experimental-based estimating approaches involve the developer performing a small amount of actual work on the project and then stopping, measure progress, and then projecting the effort needed to complete the entire project. Experimental approaches are popular with iterative and incremental development (I-I) methods such as agile development.

In agile development, there are no tasks or processes nor almost any recognizable development terms. Agile developers like a clean terminology slate and invest inordinate amounts of time coming up with new words for old ideas. For example, they have replaced the work breakdown structure (WBS) *task,* and the object technology *use case* with the agile *story* (an end-user oriented function). Each story is assigned a complexity number, called a *story point* usually between two and eight, although other scales exist. The project kicks off before any effort estimates are generated. Each team tackles a story turning user requirements into executable code. When a story is complete, the effort needed to create it is calculated. The effort required for the first few completed stories is then used to develop a standard for assessing the effort required to complete the remaining stories. For example, imagine a project consisting of 40 stories: 10 two-point stories, 20 four-point stories, and 10 eight-point stories. If it takes an average of 2 team-weeks to complete each of the first three four-point stories, then the team can estimate that it should take approximately 34 team-weeks to complete the 17 remaining four-point stories.

How do you estimate the effort for an agile project before completing any work? Well you could look at past projects, although many agile enthusiasts believe that story effort is team dependent, meaning that the effort-per-story required by one team is not applicable to any other teams.

Iterative and incremental development approaches such as agile development have the same problem as the traditional approaches (such as the waterfall approach)—there is still the problem of a credible Day 1 project estimate.

The Sad Truth

How good are these approaches? Well, they all require a *seed*, and that is where things get sticky. A *seed* can be a concept or a number that is the starting point for an estimating technique. SLIM requires data on successfully completed development projects, which are entered into the SLIM model. COCOMO requires an estimate of the number of lines of code in the completed system. Function Point Analysis requires estimating the number of end-user functions the system will contain. Delphi requires the experience of a few experts to start the more formal effort estimating cycle. The experimental approach requires the completion of a number of use cases or stories before any estimate is possible.

Do these systems work? It depends on the quality of the *seed* A starting point for an estimating technique. In most cases a number varying from randomly selected to an educated guess to kick-off an estimating process. Good seed, good estimate, bad seed, unfortunately, typical estimate. Why is the seed so often bad? Because it is an estimate! So to derive a good estimate we need a good estimate to start the whole process—a Catch-22.

But there is hope; we just have to come up with a better seed.

Building a Nuclear Missile Using the Three Bears Problem

The Project Evaluation and Review Technique (PERT), developed by Booz Allen Hamilton and others for the U.S. Navy's Polaris missile project, applies an interesting approach to this problem. PERT primarily focuses on estimating the time it takes to complete a project. It requires not one, but three estimates: *optimistic, pessimistic,* and *most likely,* representing the minimum possible time, the best estimate, and the maximum possible time required, respectively, to complete the project (the three bears of estimating). Technically, PERT focuses on time not effort; however, the technique is routinely used to estimate effort as well.

This is how it works. The three estimates are added together, and the average becomes the "official" estimate. For example, assume that the the estimates to complete a new system are 70 person-months, 80 person-months, and 110 person-months, representing the optimistic, most likely, and pessimistic efforts. Add the three together and divide by three and the result, called the *expected* effort, is 86.7 person-months.

Most PERT aficionados multiply the *most likely* effort by a factor of three or four, giving it more weight. Using the most popular factor of four, then the result is a calculated *expected* effort of 83.3 person-months. (Yes, an interesting peccadillo of PERT is that the end result is not called the *most likely* effort but rather the *expected* effort.)

The good news about PERT is that it at least talks about pessimistic estimates. The bad news is that PERT teams underestimate effort by almost as much as non-PERT teams. Although PERT points out a number of important issues, it does not solve the much deeper problem.

For Whom the Bell Curve Tools

How tall is the average person in a town? Assume we measure all the adults in town and get a variety of measurements ranging from less than 5 feet to near 7 feet with an average around 67 inches. This spread is a called a *distribution*. If the distribution is symmetrical, that is if the individual measurements cluster around the particular number and then trail off equally on both sides, then the distribution is said to be normal (ignoring the more stringent mathematical definition). If you plot all of the measurements, you get a graph that looks like the one in Figure 5.1.

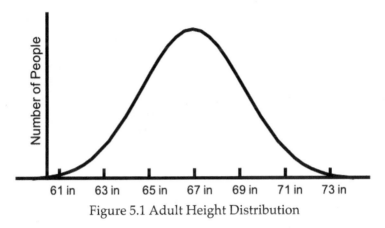

Figure 5.1 Adult Height Distribution

The graph shows that the average height is about 67 inches and that there are many more people who are 69 inches than 71 inches. If we define height down to the last decimal place, we can say that half of all the people in the sample are shorter than 67.000000000 inches and half are taller. A *normal distribution* says that the rate of difference is mirrored on the shorter and taller sides. Just as many people are 2 inches taller as are 2 inches shorter than the norm, as are the number of people 4 inches taller and shorter. The distribution, dispersion, or variation of the left side of the curve mirrors that on the right side of the curve.

The plot of a *normal distribution* is referred to as a *Gaussian distribution*, after its discoverer Johann Gauss, or a *bell curve*, after its shape.

Bell curves crop up everywhere. Paint manufacturers know that home owners painting the exterior of their houses often miscalculate how many gallons of paint they will need, buying either more or less paint than required. Purchases, in neighborhoods of identical houses might range from 4 to 12 gallons, while the required amount is 8 gallons, resulting in a normal distribution curve similar to the one in Figure 5.1, where the number and spread of underestimation of paint needed mirrors the number and spread of those who overestimated.

It would be reasonable to expect that project effort estimating follows the same pattern—that the number and distribution of underestimates mirror the number and distribution of the overestimates.

Figure 5.2 is a bell curve, where the y-axis is the number of projects and the x–axis is percent divergence from the original estimate (forecast). If this is a normal distribution, then project actual effort will cluster around the forecast. Because we can add as many decimal places as we want, we should expect that the actual effort for half (50 percent) of the projects should be less than the forecast, and we should expect the actual effort for half (50 percent) of the projects to be greater than the forecast. To make this example a little more real world, we will equate effort estimate with budget such that a project that underestimates effort can be said to be over-budget, while a project that overestimates effort can be said to be underbudget.

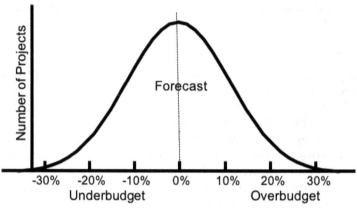

Figure 5.2 Expected Effort Distribution

However, when we plot the actuals, we get an unpleasant surprise. (Figure 5.3).

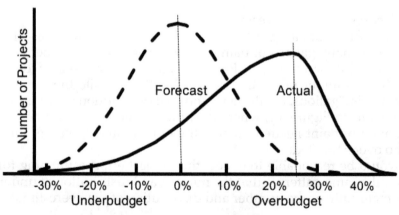

Figure 5.3 Expected vs. Actual Effort Distribution

In spite of all the estimating approaches, all the estimating techniques, all the estimating tools, and all the estimating gurus, the results are uneven. More projects come in overbudget than underbudget. Researcher after researcher reports that the majority of completed projects underestimated effort—either it costs more than they estimated or it took longer to complete than planned, or both.

One would expect the overbudgets to roughly equal the underbudgets, but they don't. Something else is going on, but what?

Falling Into the Gene Pool?

Who knows. Maybe someday some evolutionary biologist will discover the *underestimation gene*—the chromosome that causes our species to underestimate any and every task. Why might we have such a gene? Maybe, back in our primordial past, if we had really understood how difficult some things were we would never have undertaken them.

Imagine how history would be different if our recently tree-dwelling ancestor said, "I think I'll invent the wheel today," only to have his neighbor one cave over say, "Don't forget that you need to figure out how to reduce the friction created between the hub and the axle, and how are you going to make the wheel perfectly round?" It would seem inevitable that our discouraged ancestor would put wheel-inventing off for another day.

Luckily for us, our creative ancestors might have been too stupid to know how difficult most things were. Unhampered by the realities of the situation, they plowed ahead building that wheel—although probably late and overbudget.

This useful skill of underestimating effort might have been passed down generation to generation so that now the do-it-yourselfer thinks he can single-handedly build that shed in a week or assemble that bookshelf in the directions-predicted 2 hours. Unfinished sheds and weeklong bookshelf assembly might be a testimony to our genetic past—we attempt it because we're too stupid to know better. Our estimation-challenged brains don't see the potential problems, but only a perfect result. We mistakenly envision that every board of that shed is squarely cut and to the correct length, every nail goes straight in, every upright and horizontal is plumb, every join is tight. Our fixated minds might not envision sloppy sawing, poorly aimed hammers, sloping walls, skinned knees, bruised elbows, or three stitches across the forehead from a hostile beam.

How many times have you heard the refrain, "If I had only known how hard it was going to be, I never would have started it"? However, the *underestimation gene*, if it exists, might be the cause of almost every great human advance—driving the undertaking of tasks simply because we did not know how hard they would be. The implications of any hypothesized *underestimation gene* would certainly extend to project estimation. Short of gene therapy, what is a project manager to do?

The sad results, but reality of the situation, is that whatever you do, you are destined (doomed?), by some lack of knowledge, or some Area 51 experiment gone awry, or perhaps by some aberrant gene, to underestimate the effort required to build your system. Be forewarned. This is the *estimation conundrum*. The systems development Kobayashi Maru. The no-win scenario.

WHAT YOU CAN DO

Perfectam consilium (planning for the perfect) is the realization that when one estimates the effort of anything, in the estimator's mind is the picture of how the effort will unfold *if everything goes perfectly*. Estimators won't say it and they will deny it if confronted with it, because they honestly don't know they are doing it; but the *under-estimation gene*, or whatever, is making them focus on unrealistic expectations that result in gross underestimates.

Making the Prefect Real—Or at Least as Real as It Can Be

What is a project manager to do? Well based on the previous pages of misery, there are three things project manager should do.

Every Project Manager Should Be Familiar With, and Use, Multiple Estimating Techniques

First, understand what the best minds in the business have to say. There are dozens of estimating methods and hundreds of books the project manager can read. Read the books, study the methods, but remember, experience tells us that even with all this knowledge in your brain, your estimates will stink just as bad as they did before— well maybe not as bad (and that is the good news). If the experts and the experienced have difficulty estimating what does that say about the rest of us?

Anyone who is a project manager, responsible for estimating, or will be held to estimates made by others, should be familiar with a number of the major and most popular estimating approaches, techniques, and tools. The smart estimator will use more than one approach/technique and maybe even more than one tool to arrive at the best estimate possible. Such knowledge and actions should at least reduce the vicissitude and inexactness of estimating, and, in the worst case provide some cover of *plausible deniability*—both IT and user management want to see that you used scientific and accepted approaches to arrive at your poor estimates.

Every Project Manager Should Have Detailed Knowledge of the Organization's Systems Development History

The project manager should also have access to people who have detailed knowledge of the organization's systems development history; or have access to systems development documentation.

Even if the project books have been so well cooked they should be served on a bun, the people who cooked the books might be quite useful. What a team member might not document on paper, he or she might be willing to share with a fellow developer, detailing the ugly challenges faced by a previous project. While books and articles can talk about systems development in general, current and former developers in your organization retain a different yet equally important store of information. Experiences working with other team members, users, and management (both IT and user), the technical environment (what works and what doesn't work so well), etc. can provide the estimator with a treasure trove of useful information.

Every Project Manager Should Be Aware of **Perfectam consilium** *(the human defect that we look to the perfect not the realistic) when estimating—it's in our nature*

When all is said and done, the estimator needs to sit down and apply some rational thought. Use the charts and the math, talk to users, other developers and team members to develop estimates. However, the last step is one of realistic reflection on human nature.

Not fudging data, or SWAG (systematic wild-assed guess), but rather a well thought out rational realization of the human condition to *plan for the prefect*. Make sure that you add the real to the perfect.

The better solution is not to fight human nature. If we are predisposed to always *plan for the perfect*, that is, if all of our estimates are *ideal estimates*, then maybe we should not fight it but rather go with it. Accept that our forecasts are all *ideal estimates* and learn to adjust accordingly.

A Semi-Kooky Solution

The PERT people almost had it right when they divided estimates into three categories representing the *optimistic, pessimistic,* and *most likely* predictions representing the minimum possible time, the maximum possible time, and some mid-point they believed would most likely be the actual time required to complete the project. The genius of their approach was separating an estimate into optimistic and pessimistic.

Planning for the perfect leads to an *ideal estimate*, which is the traditional standard guess of how long a project will take if everything goes as it should. However, projects usually take longer—the actual is the idealistic estimate plus a factor x, which, for lack of a better term, we can call the *reality factor*. If we know the reality factor, then we can say that the most *realistic estimate* is the *ideal estimate* plus this *reality factor*. If the *ideal estimate* is that the project will take 100 person-months and the *reality factor* is 15 percent, then the *realistic estimate* is 115 person-months.

A *reality factor* is not a *fudge factor*. A *fudge factor* is an arbitrary number applied to an estimate to increase its chances of being correct. A *reality factor* (RF) is an observable modification to an *ideal estimate* (IE) to make it a *realistic estimate* (RE).

The real challenge then is to learn what is an organization's, or better yet an individual estimator's, actual *reality factor*. How do you determine a *reality factor*? Here are three approaches in order of importance.

History. Look at past projects, both original estimates and actuals. Documentation will help but it is often not enough. Scope changes, poor record keeping (especially lack of post-project reviews), and cooking the books can lead to questionable results. Better results might come from interviewing staff on those projects. Sit down with team members and go through their projects, in as much detail as you and they can stomach. Promise anonymity, but get as real a picture as possible of project variances.

Literature. Academics and project management gurus often publish articles containing variance information.

Best Guess. The process has to start somewhere. If your organization has no useful history and you cannot find useful information searching libraries or the web, then you have to take the first step and come up with the best *reality factor* you can. This is not a *fudge factor*, but rather the hopeful start of a long personal, if not organizational, journey to devise, over time, a useful *reality factor*. Follow-through is required. The *reality factor* needs to be revisited every time actuals become available (any estimate and actuals will do, they do not have to be for an entire system—components and small efforts are OK), the actuals need to be compared with the estimate, and a revised *reality factor* created. A reliable *reality factor* should start to emerge after just a few estimates and their comparison to actuals.

It is only fitting that the solution for a half-baked concept such as the *underestimation gene* be given an equally half-baked name. With all due modesty—and that is considerable modesty—the nomination for a name for the process to abrogate the *estimation conundrum*—an imperfect method of planning—is the *Imperfect Method for Planning* or *IMP*.

A working definition of the *Imperfect Method for Planning (IMP)* might be the recognition that a *realistic estimate (RE)* for any project is: (1) the *ideal estimate* (IE), which assumes that every project task will complete without problems, on time, and on budget, plus (2) an effort adjustment calculated using a historical *reality factor* (RF), which is the percentage the *ideal estimate* needs to be modified to deliver a system that includes unanticipated interruptions, obstacles, and any other unplanned events. RE=IE+(IE*RF). (The Appendix: Post-Project Review Recalculating Project Effort and Creating a Reality Factor includes the steps for how to create your own, somewhat useful, *reality factor* (RF).)

Looking for a better way to estimate project costs? You really only have three options. One, do nothing and live with the current state of affairs. Two, accept the flawed and moderately silly IMP. approach presented here. Three, come up with a better way of estimating effort.

Dissatisfied with these answers? Get used to it. Unfortunately, this is as good as it gets and why they have to pay you to do the job.

In Summary

Project plans have always been a tug of war among user, management, and developer. Users want, sometimes insist on, unrealistic budgets and schedules, while management sometimes cares more about actuals meeting forecasts than system quality. Add to the mix project management's miserable estimation skills and the result is a witch's brew of failure.

Because the definitive project estimating approach has yet to be developed, and possibly never will be, the rational project manager or project estimator should take advantage of every archive, technique, and tool, as well as any innate proclivities, to arrive at the best possible picture of a project. They might not be pretty but, when push comes to shove, they are really all we have.

THE TAKEAWAY

- Regardless of the tool or technique used, forecasting project effort before commencing any project work is a guess, and forecasting project effort after a few project tasks are completed increases the accuracy of the forecast from guess to educated guess, but it's still a guess.

- The problem is perfectam consilium (planning for the perfect)—the realization that when one estimates the effort of anything, in the estimator's mind is a picture of how the effort will unfold *if everything goes perfectly.*

- The knowledgeable project estimator will use all the tools and techniques available and supplement them with personal experience and organizational history to understand how, in the past, reality diverged from the ideal—the *reality factor.*

- A more *realistic estimate* is the *ideal estimate* (the effort required to build a system if everything goes perfectly) plus a *reality factor* (the historical organizational systems development variance from the ideal estimate.)

- A useful *reality factor* can only be developed by examining past work to understand an individual estimator's or an IT organization's underestimation history.

PART TWO

GETTING THE PROJECT STARTED

Chapter 6

Screwing Up Staffing
or
Staff, the Bread of Project Life

Thy staff they comfort me.
~ Psalms

Go to any IT conference or class, and you see the attendees chatting with each other about their organization's hardware, software, networks, tools, methods, and techniques. But you almost never hear them talk about their staff. What is surprising about this is that study after study has shown that among all the assets at IT's command—hardware, software, networks, tools, techniques, methods, and staff—staff is the most important. Countless academic studies from every corner of the globe, consistently over the past 50 years, have shown that staff are the number one factor in determining project success. The better your staff are the less important are the other IT assets.

Take productivity. Studies of programmers within the same organization have shown that the most productive programmer is often ten or more times more productive than the least productive programmer. And, because it is rare for the best in an organization to be paid more than twice the worst, they are a bargain. The same is also true for analysts and designers, with the most productive far out-producing the least productive.

There was an interesting example of this in the 1970s and 1980s. Unlike now, when just a few companies dominate the computer landscape, then there were literally dozens and dozens of minicomputer manufacturers. Most of them designed and supported their own chipset with their own operating system, assembler language, etc. Each new chipset required rewriting the operating system—an onerous task for many of these companies, which tended to focus on hardware (the "iron") much more than the software. The many different ways these minicomputer companies developed similar systems provides some interesting, though anecdotal, conclusions about development styles.

Unscientific observation uncovered two basic philosophies for operating systems development. The first was to hire a large number of rather average staff (50, 75, or more) and then split the job among numerous sub-teams. Each sub-team would complete its small task and hand it off to another team, which integrated it into the formal system. This was known as the Mongolian horde approach.

The second philosophy called for hiring just a handful (three to eight) exceptionally talented programmers who wrote the entire system. This was a variation of the chief programmer team concept (single chief surrounded by a few supporters) which, arguably, is the great grandfather of many of the development approaches of today. Call this the small expert team approach.

A very unscientific look at their output showed that the small team of experts did a better job (tighter code, fewer errors, more flexible and a more maintainable system) than the systems developed by the horde. The lesson to be learned is that a few very talented people, who know what they are doing, beat the mob of common folk every time. That was the lesson. The moral of the story is different. Find, acquire, and keep the very talented as long as you can. They make everyone look good.

Staff Productivity

The natural starting point for any discussion of productivity would be to define it. This is not an easy task and some very brilliant IT researchers are bald from scratching their heads for the past few decades trying to do just that.

If you review the business literature, productivity definitions center on the concept of the output (work produced) divided by the input (assets consumed). Some systems developers define productivity as the amount of work completed (lines of code, functions analyzed, modules developed, programs tested, stories completed, etc.) in a unit of time (because most IT costs, even computer usage, can be monetized as time consumed). What is nice about these definitions is that they are very mathematical. There is no problem applying a factor to one knowing the impact on the other. Double the time and the amount of work is doubled. Halve the time and half the work is completed. Its mathematical nature makes it a very popular definition. However, this definition assumes that productivity consists of two variables, work and time. What is missing is a very important third variable.

Imagine two programmers A and B, each producing 1,000 lines of workable code (LOC) in 40 hours. The output is the same, 1,000 LOC, and the resources consumed are the same, 40 hours, but the work of A might be qualitatively superior to the work of B. The third and missing variable in our productivity definition is *quality*. Contrary to Joseph Stalin (who is reported to have said that "quantity has a quality all its own"), quality is not quantifiable, at least no one has come up with a popular quantifiable definition of systems development quality.

Though there is difficulty in defining *quality*, some understanding of the word is needed for any intelligent discussion of systems development productivity. One is left with U.S. Supreme Court Justice Potter Steward's comment who, when speaking about pornography, said that he couldn't define it, "but I know it when I see it." If the definition of software quality is left to what we commonly observe, then most would probably agree with the following. Quality (software) is code that: (1) meets or exceeds standards of form and structure, (2) meets or exceeds all functional (user) requirements, (3) contains no serious errors, (4) is well documented, and (5) is easily understandable by other experienced coders.

Note that by adding *quality* to the definition of *productivity* one has to give up the ability to do simple arithmetic on productivity. That is unfortunate, but until some researcher can remedy the situation, applying the *quality* variable to project planning will be rather difficult.

For the purpose of this chapter, and to keep our hair (at least as much was we have left), we will use this simple working definition. Productivity is the amount of *quality* work completed by a team member or team in a unit of time.

This definition might be disappointing without its mathematical neatness, but it contains at least a grain of truth. Everybody knows people in IT who are different producers. Some produce work quickly while other take forever. Some produce high-quality work while others...well just be glad they don't work for an aircraft or heart pacemaker manufacturer.

What every project manager should want on his or her team is the most productive (quality work produced in a reasonable amount of time) staff possible.

THE PROBLEM

How do you get productive staff? Hire them? Grow them? Poach them?

The problem is so simple, yet so real. If you want first rate systems, then you need first rate staff. Conversely, if your staff isn't first rate, your systems won't be either. If staff quality is the number one factor in project success, one would think that acquiring and maintaining quality staff would the the number one priority in every IT organization. But it isn't.

The problem is a lack of *sufficient* IT involvement is the selection and development of IT staff. Unfortunately, IT staff acquisition and development is usually relegated to one or two "human resources" (HR) people in IT, if not completely outsourced to a non-IT human resources department.

WHAT YOU CAN DO

For many IT organizations the project manager has little say about the productivity, training, or experience of project staff. They are given X people at the beginning of the project and that is that. Only a few project managers have a say regarding the skills of their team members, much less exactly who they are. Hiring and training are traditionally reserved for IT and increasingly HR. Staffing (assigning people to a project) is still an IT task but about which project managers traditionally have had little say. So the question becomes, what is this chapter about?

IT might hold most of the people-management cards but that does not mean that an industrious project manager cannot influence the process.

Hiring Staff

Hiring productive people is the best and cheapest way for IT to gain productive staff. Unfortunately, it is also the area where IT does the worst job of gaining exceptional people. Why? Because the system is geared to hire the average and not the exceptional.

Look at the typical IT hiring practice, which focuses on formal education; experience, usually defined as time served in their last title (such as analyst, lead programmer, network administrator, etc.); computer languages, tools, and techniques they know; criminal background check; and drug test. Productivity is not even mentioned. Worse, because HR is increasingly taking over all hiring functions, a technical/professional assessment of candidate productivity is highly unlikely. Too often HR's candidate screening is limited to word matching—lining up the words in IT's staff request with those on a candidate's resume. ("Oh, you know C++. Too bad, we were looking for a C programmer.") Lastly, IT salaries, routinely analyzed, plotted, and graphed by HR, are forcefully structured toward the average in the industry. Average salaries acquire average staff, not exceptional staff. This is a case where *average* is just another word for *mediocre*.

Because there are no good measurements of productivity (remember the quality thing?), the only way to gauge a job candidate's skills is for the most talented IT staff to spend time with the candidate discussing his or her knowledge, experience, and that *je ne sais quoi* that sets apart the talented.

Is this a good process for hiring the productive? Maybe. However, it's better than anything else that is even remotely in the typical IT hiring process.

What a Project Manager Can Do

IT's problem is mirrored by the project team. Many project managers either have no say or do not challenge who is on their team. However, every project manager should want the best staff on his or her team and should be willing to make sure it happens. A little two-step process will help. First, do what IT should have done, interview all prospective team members with a special eye for productivity. Be very selective. Second, as best as you can, gain from IT management the right to accept or reject staff. This is not always easy because it might fly in the face of IT policy, but it is worth trying. Be willing to compromise, because even settling for less than you want is better than just accepting what you are given.

Determining who is on your team and who will have a significant input to your professional success, should be job one.

Hiring People Smarter Than You

A customer was suing a software vendor because the vendor's billing software did not accurately reflect sales. The complaint was filed by a newspaper chain. No matter what one of their their papers did, their advertising billing system would not tally with cash, and at the same time, customers were complaining about double and triple billing.

No one on the vendor programming team could figure out the problem—their code worked perfectly in their office and with other clients. In desperation, the programming manager hired a former newspaper business manager, at a salary greater than his own, to figure out what was going on. The business manager studied the software and the procedures at the newspaper and determined that the accounting processes at the paper were at fault. Further, she laid out what changes the newspaper should make not only to make the software tally correctly but, for the first time, to give the paper an accurate picture of its ad sales.

The programming manager was so impressed, he made his new employee oversee the quality of not only the software his team produced but to review the office practices of their clients to ensure that the marriage of systems and office processes worked perfectly.

Some vendor executives were uncomfortable having a manager make less than one of his subordinates. However, the manager was very happy because the new, high-priced, employee made him and the rest of the team look good.

The moral of the story is that regardless of the makeup of the team the manager gets the credit for the good work the team does as well as the blame for the poor work they do. Hiring an employee smarter, more experienced, or even higher paid, reflects positively on the manager, not negatively. The simple fact is that the best way for managers to look good is to hire and have the best people work for them.

Training Staff

Training is not foreign to the IT industry, which prides itself on the amount of classroom time provided staff. The question is, how well spent are those training dollars?

Team Member Training

Hiring an entire department of superstars is unrealistic. The most many IT shops can hope for is to recruit a few exceptional people. For the majority of IT organizations, any hope of gaining exceptional developers will come from training and in-house provided experience.

IT spends considerable sums of money on training—much of it wasted. For many organizations, training is treated as a staff benefit not a department asset. Courses are selected based on employee interest rather than IT need. When an analyst does well on an assignment or on her annual review, she is rewarded with 5 days in sunny southern California at a data-flow diagramming class. Why data-flow diagramming? Is that an IT needed skill? Is there a project that will be starting shortly where data-flow diagramming will be key?

Few IT organizations tie training to an overall staffing plan or master project schedule. However, training is needed for staff to do just a passable job on a small project, much less on a large one.

Once again, HR or a corporate training department, is increasingly responsible for all corporate training, including IT's. Though many HR departments do a decent job for the average IT employee, they almost never have the training the exceptional developer needs. Sending IT's best people to a "C++ for C Programmers," course might be a waste of their time.

What a Project Manager Can Do

The project manager often has to live with IT's reward-based training philosophy while making the best of this less-than-ideal situation. All the project manager can do is to fill any gap before project kickoff with appropriate project-focused training. For example, if there is a time lag between when first presented with the idea of the project and its kickoff, have IT management fill that time period with needed training. Those dollars are not wasted. Even if the project is never funded you at least managed to provide staff with appropriate training.

The project manager can also influence the training of IT staff not currently on any project. Gather all of IT's project managers together and discuss any organizational skill gaps; then, create a list of the training the group feels the organization needs. Present it to IT management as a constructive suggestion.

IT Manager Training

Training IT managers in the use of project tools and techniques is not enough. They also need important, often missing, skills. Given that the near universal finding by researchers that staff is the most important IT asset for project success, it is surprising that very few IT managers are trained in skills focused on staff hiring and staff personal development. One would think that developing hiring skills (interviewing, researching backgrounds, assessing need and fit) and bolstering the skills of existing employees (understanding both the employees' and IT's development needs and how to satisfy them) would be at the top of the list. Unfortunately, it is not even *on the list* in most IT shops.

Ideally IT should go further. Rather than providing hiring and staff development skills to managers (line and project); competence in screening, interviewing, evaluating, and hiring staff should be a required skill to be promoted to manager. However, that nirvana is way off in the future. For the present, it would be great if IT organizations simply aided existing managers in acquiring these skills.

HR can take the lead in placing advertising, collecting and managing applications, and pre-screening applicants, but they are HR and not IT people. It is unfair to require that they know all that is needed to hire good IT staff. IT needs to be an active participant in all phases of the process. HR can and should play a major role in staff hiring but that does not mean that IT can abdicate its responsibility.

What a Project Manager Can Do

This can be a difficult problem for the project manager. No one wants to tell his or her boss that he or she can use additional training. Their legitimate concern is that it's tantamount to saying to IT management that you are not qualified to lead a project. However, if you feel skills are wanting or should be sharpened, then you need to speak up. Most, though not all, IT managers will applaud your honesty and approve the proper training.

The Project Manager Group

Accountants, corporate training staff, even custodial staff often meet as a group to discuss their common concerns. Project managers? Not so much. Maybe it is an idea whose time has come.

In many, if not most, IT shops, management selects the systems development tools, techniques, training materials, methods, etc. However, it is the project managers who have the collective knowledge of what works best. The entire IT organizations could benefit if project managers met, shared their experiences, their solutions, even their horror stories.

Meet in the office or at your local watering hole after work, but get those who manage the building of systems together to share, learn, even commiserate with each other. Everyone will benefit.

Don't forget books or online courses. You don't always need a formal course to learn needed skills, and these can be taken on the QT.

Staff Experience

Do you know the difference between a client and a consumer? Both are customers, but they are viewed differently by the business world and treated quite distinctly. A consumer is someone who walks into a store and buys a product (pack of gum) or a service (dry cleaning a shirt). The interaction between the vendor and the customer is transactional, meaning that it has a defined start and end, exists for only a short period of time, and is independent of any other interactions. When it's over, it's over. A client is a customer who has an ongoing relationship with the vendor, possibly over decades. Vendors have been known to forgo shorter-term (consumer-like) sales if the transaction is not viewed positively for the longer-term (client-like) relationship. Accountants, lawyers, and drug dealers consider their customers to be clients.

The important takeaway from this discussion of IT staff is how successful vendors treat their clients. They are in the relationship for the long run, so they do not let the possible gain from a single sale or interaction interfere with the longer-term relationship.

How does IT treat IT project staffing? Like a vending machine comes to mind. Whoever does project staffing looks to see who is available and then pulls the lever on the best candidates. The entire process is transactional—the shorter–term consumer model—and not geared toward the longer-term client model. The enlightened IT organization has an experience plan for each IT member. Placing system-developer A on project B might make the most sense for the project but it might not be the right move for employee A or for IT in the long run.

Placing an employee on a project solely for the benefit of the employee is just as wrong as placing the employee on a project solely for the benefit of the project. IT needs to ensure that the right balance of employee and project benefit is met.

What a Project Manager Can Do

This is a case where the project manager can, once again, mimic what IT does, or should do. Many if not most project teams are transactional—they are assembled for a particular project and then disbanded once the project is complete. However, exceptional project managers have a group of people they work with again and again. The neophyte project manager should try to develop a cohort of staff who work together whenever possible. This allows every one of the team to know each other's experience, supplement needed skills, and do so efficiently and effectively.

The same client mentality can be applied to the user community. Project managers should strive to know their clients (users) by meeting with them frequently; attending their meetings and gatherings, if invited; and sharing common news and trends, such how new technology is affecting their business areas, etc.—even if no common project is underway or scheduled. Develop a real relationship with the client before any planned projects.

Hiring, Training, and Experience...Oh My!

Asking which of the three—hiring the best staff, providing useful training, or helping the staff member gain experience—is the most important is the wrong question. The smart money is on doing all three. A sound hiring policy might not always give you the most productive people, but it can lead to you hiring the most motivated. The most motivated employees will gain the most from training. Training will help staff do a good job on a number of small projects, while experience on small projects will qualify them for working on the large, important, business mission-critical projects. That is win, win, win; a win for the project, a win for the business users, and a win for the individual IT staff members.

IT managers need to have the skills to hire the best people, develop them while they are employees, and keep them within the firm. Hiring, developing, and keeping are skills that are just as easily taught as programming, sensitivity training, and timesheet management; they are just not as available. Few organizations do this, and the trend is in the wrong direction as more and more IT shops turn staff assessment and development tasks over to a corporate HR department.

What a Project Manager Can Do

Project managers can act in a similar way to IT managers. Staffing a project is analogous to IT hiring staff. First, if you can, gain from IT the right to pick your own team. It might be culturally difficult in your organization—then again, it might not be. You won't know until you ask.

Second, by the time a project kicks off it might be too late for at least some staff training. However, you can better prepare staff for the next project. Have all the project managers meet and identify needed IT skills, then take the group recommendation to IT management.

Third, staff experience can be accelerated by having teams that work well together. People comfortable with each other are more likely to help teammates gain and use needed skills, jumpstarting the experience curve.

THE TAKEAWAY

- Study after study has shown that the most critical component for systems development success is staff.
  - Research shows that for the average IT organization, its most productive programmer is often more than ten times more productive than its least productive programmer. The same is true for analysts, designers, and testers.

- — Because the salaries of the most to least productive staff rarely exceed two to one, the most productive/expensive staff provides the most bang for the buck.
- — Unfortunately, IT managers are rarely trained in hiring the exceptional, in further developing them once they are hired, and keeping them satisfied with their jobs.

- There are a few things the project manager can do to energize his or her project team.
  - — The project manager can approach project staffing the same way IT approaches or should approach hiring—look for the best and most productive staff.
  - — All of IT's project managers should be involved with IT's overall training plan (assuming it has one) recommending needed courses, tools, classes, etc.
  - — Staff experience can be accelerated by building ongoing teams of people who often work together.

Chapter 7

The Fungible Fallacy
or
Fun with Fungibles

This is the dimension of imagination.
It is an area which we call the Twilight Zone.
~ Rod Serling

Is IT an art or a science? Should IT staffing be grounded in math or formal systems? Practitioners seem to be happy leaving these questions to philosophers. Few systems developers spend much time trying to determine whether they are scientists, mathematicians, engineers, or artists.

We do like numbers though, and we like to include them in our reports to management. Basically, we like to count things. We count users, computers, programs, lines of code, errors, dollars and, one of the coolest things to count, people. We can calculate how many people are needed on a project, what each person will produce, how long it will take them to do it, and even what they cost, all without knowing who they are. The power of math makes individual team member experience and skills unimportant. At least that is how the project planning process works.

Person-Month

One of the nice intersections of the worlds of IT and business is people counting—how many people on the payroll, how many staff in Chicago, and how many people needed to develop a system. We use terms such as *person-month* (rather than man-month, because we are not gauche chauvinist pigs), which allows us to apply some primitive math to people. What is nice about *person-month* is that it is not only countable but you can apply arithmetic operators to it. For example, 10 person-months is half of 20 person-months. Assuming all the arithmetic gods are properly aligned, then a project requiring 100 person-months can be completed in 10 months if the project is staffed with 10 people and completed in 5 months if staffed with 20 people.

Full-Time Equivalent (FTE)

If *person-month* is the left hand of counting people, then *full-time equivalent* is the right. *Full-time equivalent* (FTE) expresses how many full-time people will be needed to do something.

Full-Time Equivalent

There are many definitions of Full-Time Equivalent (FTE), most of them terrible. The gist of these definitions is that an FTE is the ratio of the actual hours a team member works compared with hours defined as full-time.

There is a simpler definition. FTE equals a virtual team member.

One FTE theoretically produces the work of one full-time team member. Where FTEs become important is with part-time staff. For example, imagine a project requiring five full-time people for 2 months. However, you can only staff four full-time team members for the first month and three for the second. By adding two half-time team members for the first month and four half-time team members for the second month, you then have a fully staffed (five FTE) project. Note that the headcount for the first month is actually six and seven for the second month even though both months have five FTEs.

You can think of using FTEs in two different ways. The first is dividing up a team member's responsibility. For example, if an analyst spends 50 percent of her time meeting with users, 30 percent conferring with team members, 10 percent doing administrative tasks such as writing reports and meeting with project management, and 10 percent conducting systems analysis training of other team members, then the job could be categorized as one-half FTE meeting with users, three-tenth FTE meeting with team members, one-tenth FTE doing admin, and one-tenth FTE training. If the project manager wants to have the analyst work 60 percent with users, then he needs to reassign the one-tenth FTE training task to other staff.

The second use of FTEs is to determine actual headcount and costs. By identifying the effort required for every project task, the project manager can easily determine the number of FTEs required for the entire project as well as the staffing costs. The number of FTEs also gives you a minimum headcount requirement. For example:

TASK	EFFORT (person-months)
Analysis	100
Design	90
Coding	60
Testing	120
Installation/conversion	20
TOTAL	390 person-months

At $10,000 a person-month, project staffing will cost $3,900,000. To complete the project in 10 months will require 39 FTEs, but only 24.375 FTEs if the schedule can be extended to 16 months.

But there is one more item needed to tie this whole thing together.

Fungibility

Person-months and FTEs work because of a concept called *fungibility*. Fungible refers to an asset that can be substituted with another asset of the same kind. Fungible objects have no individuation and are interchangeable with all other objects of the same class. For example, US dollars are fungible. If someone owes you 10 dollars then any 10 dollars (any 10-dollar bill, or two 5-dollar bills, or 40 quarters, you get the idea) will do.

In terms of people, fungibility means that one staff member equals two half-time staff and four quarter-time staff. Fungibility is the mechanism that allows the IT manager as well as the project manager to exercise his or her extensive counting skills and translate FTEs into headcount.

Then again, maybe not.

THE PROBLEM

You often hear in a movie or read in a novel the refrain, "Put more men on the job." The phrase punctuates some confrontation between management (usually portrayed as the bad guy) and the lowly foreman trying to make the best of an almost impossible situation. The implication is that by adding bodies to the project it will happen faster or at least get done.

Taking the Fun Out of Fungible

Years ago, Fredrick Brooks, in his monumental book, *The Mythical Man-Month*, confronted the fallacy of just adding bodies to a job to make it finish sooner, showing that, in fact, added staff can actually further slowdown progress. That insight led to Brooks', installment in the IT pantheon of wisdom.

The Addition Fallacy

Brooks is right. When a project is in trouble and there is risk of missing a deadline, putting additional staff on a project can actually slow it down rather than speed it up. For example, if a 50 person-month project with a staff of ten is 2 months behind schedule, adding five more staff might cause them to become 3 months behind schedule. The math simple doesn't work. Why?

Many reasons. For example, the existing staff have to stop the critical project work they are doing to get the new staff up to speed. Also, numerous studies show that larger teams require more coordination and communication than smaller teams, with the additional necessary time taken away from project work.

The need for team members to consult with each other is called *communication overhead* and should be a part of the overall project cost in time and effort. Brooks and others have pointed out that as staff are added to a project, the communication overhead soars, with some reporting an exponential increase. All of that additional time and effort has to be accounted for, but usually isn't. The result? You guessed it—the situation goes from bad to worse.

However, the issue goes beyond adding more staff to an existing project. Rather it raises the awkward question, can you treat staff as fungible?

The Partial-Person Problem

A partial FTE is just what it sounds like: a half-FTE is the equivalent of a half-time person, or two quarter-time people or four eighth-time people, etc. It can be thought of in two ways, either one real person doing the job of multiple partial FTEs or multiple part-time people doing the job of one full-time person. In the analyst example earlier in the chapter, one person spent 50 percent of her time meeting with users, 30 percent conferring with team members, 10 percent doing administrative tasks such as writing reports and meeting with management, and 10 percent conducting systems analysis training of other team members—one FTE and a headcount of one. However, if staffing is just a math problem, then the job could have just as easily been staffed by a half-time person for the analysis work, a person at 30 percent working with team members, and two 10-percent staff working on admin and training—one FTE and a headcount of four.

The effort should be the same but, owing to communication overhead, it is not. The four people will require more effort and/or more time than the single person doing all the jobs. The problem with FTEs in general and partial FTE specifically is that the reality often does not match the math.

The Interchangeable Fallacy

Most projects follow a simple sequence of events: first they are proposed, then planned, then funded, and then, when the project is ready to commence, staffed. Virtually all project planning takes place before the project manager knows who will be staffed on the project and their skills, experience, and salaries. Yet costs and schedules are needed before funding—what's a project manager to do?

Most organizations use a standard (cost) model. It might be generic cost such as all IT staff have a loaded cost of $10,000 per month, or some models are title specific such as: analysts $11,000 per month, designers $10,000 per month, programmers $8,000 per month, project managers $15,000 per month, etc. Standard models, even title specific ones, assume that all staff have the same skill level, the same experience, are equally productive, and are paid the same. However, this is never true. Staff skills, experience, productivity, and salaries vary considerably in the typical organization, making standard models problematic. For example, Chapter 6 Screwing Up Staffing points out that programmer productivity can vary more than ten-fold within the same organization. In almost every case, the project manager does not know exactly who will be assigned to the project, what skills they will have, how productive they are, and what they will cost. Therefore, accurate projected numbers cannot be baked into the plan. These uncertainties do serious damage to the notion that IT staff are fungible.

The Availability Fallacy

So far the subject is IT staff, but most projects also have a number of users assigned to the team. Many of the user staff are not assigned full-time. Business managers are reluctant to give up their best people to a project and instead either assign the less experienced staff or limit the amount of time expert user staff can spend of the project. User staff might be limited to 8, 4, or even 2 hours a week to a project meaning that project team members might have to wait days for answers to important questions. Worse, it is not at all uncommon for part-time user staff (who are forced to split their time among multiple unrelated tasks) to shave hours from project work in favor of their primary responsibility.

WHAT YOU CAN DO

It is a grave error is to assume that a person is a person is a person—that staff are interchangeable. Person-month/FTE math only works if staff are fungible and, as we have shown, they are not. So why does IT put so much emphasis on FTEs and fungibility? The answer is that IT has little choice because project costs and schedules are often required months before a project starts.

This does not mean that concepts such as person-month and FTE are not useful. In fact, they are, but only at the right time and in the right context. During project proposal or early stages of project planning, they are often the only means for providing senior management with a ball-park estimate of project costs and schedules. However, they are only useful as a starting point. As soon as actual staff assignments are known, then the project manager can start to provide more credible numbers.

It is important that the tentativeness of the project plan, with its FTE-driven budget, be known for what it is—a first-blush look at costs. The project manager, ideally with the help of IT management and the project champion (see Chapter 8 No Project Champion) needs to—

- Explain to the senior user management that the pre-kickoff project plan reflects standard and not real costs and productivity.

- Review the project plan shortly after kickoff and possibly adjust it to reflect actual project staffing.

Will senior business management go along with this Day-2 project plan review? Maybe not, but even if they do not, at least the project manager has gone on record raising the issue. At the very least, it should help at your court martial.

THE TAKEAWAY

- Concepts such as FTE and staff fungibility, and the arithmetic associated with them, are useful for estimating costs and schedules before a project starts.

- Team members are individuals with their own training, experience, and productivity, making concepts such as FTE and fungibility almost useless for a staffed project.

- Communication overhead—the resources consumed to keep team members informed—increases exponentially as the project headcount increases potentially playing havoc with costs and schedules.

- Once project staffing is finalized, the project manager should review the project plan to determine whether any staffing decisions affect project costs or schedules.

Chapter 8

No Project Champion
or
They're Not Just for Breakfast Anymore

An idea is worth nothing if it has no champion.
~ Unknown

In Franz Kafka's book *The Trial*, the protagonist is arrested for a crime unknown to him. He is not informed of when the trial will take place, who is trying him, what his crime is, how he can defend himself, or the verdict. The entire bureaucracy, its members, meetings, and decisions, are secret. He must merely wait for a punishment that will be administered with no advance warning.

It is amazing how much the bureaucracy in Kafka's *The Trial* is similar to the workings of many organizations today, both governmental and commercial.

President Andrew Jackson had an official cabinet that he tended to ignore in favor of an unofficial group of advisors dubbed the kitchen cabinet. Since then, many U.S. presidents have relied more on an unofficial list of advisors than on the official cabinet secretaries for counsel and help in making decisions. Titles can be misleading. Even recognized advisors might be marginalized while certain non-government individuals have the president's ear. Lobbyists soon learn that cozying up to the unofficial in-crowd is often more fruitful than courting official dignitaries.

Do you know who really runs that Fortune 1000 corporation? You might be surprised. Is it the board of directors? Maybe, some boards are very involved with major corporate decisions, but others are not, meeting the minimum number of times required by law, with get-togethers consisting of little more than dog and pony shows.

Sometimes the real power rests within the chain of command, with an assemblage of senior executives representing the major divisions of the organization. Other groups are less formal, with CEOs relying on an unofficial team, sometimes called an executive committee, of employees of various titles and positions, perhaps not even in the chain of command. It is these insiders who make or influence corporate decisions.

THE PROBLEM

What does this have to do with IT and project management? Many of the decisions about major IT projects, such as budgets and schedules, might be made by some committee long before any project manager is even appointed.

Put your project planning books aside. The critical decisions about your project might have been made months ago and kept secret by a group of people you don't know, sitting around a table in some unnamed conference room you never heard of, who know little to nothing about IT. Sounds like Kafka's *The Trial* doesn't it?

If you are a project manager, even the best project manager in the world, it is unlikely you will be sitting with that group anytime soon. Even the CIO might be a stranger to those assemblages.

If you are a corporate CEO and want your concerns heard by the President of the United States, then you either need a high-level White House employee on your side or need to hire an influential lobbyist. Either way, you require insiders who will look out for your interests. CEOs are not the only ones needing an insider. The same is true for project managers.

If your project is building an application to manage IT's bowling scores, then you can skip this chapter. Even the project manager of a more corporate relevant though small and not revenue significant project might be able to breeze though the following pages. However, if you project is mission critical, meaning that it plays a major role in the success of your organization, then read on, because, know it or not, your project needs a project champion.

Projects are like wolves. They are useful, play an important role in our world, have many supporters, and no matter what they do or how benign they are, they also have people who are gunning for them. Why? Who knows? For whatever reasons, someone, somewhere, will be out to get your project. He might think it's a waste of money; poorly led, planned, or executed; not needed by the business; or a better alternative is right under your nose. For whatever reason he will do all he can to bring your project to a halt. Project naysayers are usually not evil people, just convinced that a mistake is being made and that they have a responsibility to point it out if not correct it.

If the naysayer is a junior member of the organization then there is probably no problem; however, if the project critic is a senior executive then beware. Somewhere around some bend or detour you have to take, the critic waits ready to spring on any perceived misstep or error.

When will the ambush occur? Well there are a few fairly predictable points.

First Sign of Weakness

Drop the ball, or even bobble it, and you are in trouble. A slipped schedule, budget issues, vendor not able to deliver what you want or when you want, and staffing problems are all reasons the viability of the project could be questioned.

Wrong Place, Wrong Time

When a project kicks off, there is considerable enthusiasm and energy aimed at the undertaking. The project team is charged, users are thinking of how things will be when the systems is in, and managers everywhere are looking to bask in the credit they will take, deserved or not. But the enthusiasm will wane.

It doesn't matter that the plan says that the project will not show tangible user results for 8 months, or that the users were told, time and again, that there is a *deliverable desert* between months one and seven. Sometime after 3 or 4 months with nothing end-user oriented to show for all the work besides bills, even the most ardent supporters experience the *mid-project blues* and start to second-guess their decision. Now add in the naysayers whispering "I told you so" in their ears, and even the strongest supporters start rethinking the "entire project."

WHAT YOU CAN DO

There are two ways to avoid the *mid-project blues*. First, keep the drought short. Try to have something that will keep the users happy as soon and as often as possible. Never go more than 6 months before some functionality is installed, and never more than

3 months without some kind of demo. (See Chapter 9 Not Taking Advantage of the Honeymoon Period.)

Second, get a project champion. A project champion is a senior executive, usually from the business side of the organization, who has the respect of peers and juniors and the ear of the very top echelons and who truly believes in the system and the benefits it will deliver to the company.

A good project champion will keep the true believers believing and the naysayers quiet. The champion will give the project the time it needs/deserves to build the application and deliver the goods. Project champions are worth their weight in gold.

Do Not Confuse a Project Champion with a Mentor

Every project manager should have one or more mentors (official or unofficial) who can help them navigate corporate waters.

The Mentor

Mentors provide staff with advice and insight into their corporate careers, focusing on individual performance and success. Mentors can help an employee with development and training choices, positioning for promotions, interacting with other staff, etc.

If the project manager can have multiple mentors, then an excellent idea is that at least one mentor should be from outside IT with firsthand experience in how the overall organization is run.

The Project Champion

Both Six Sigma (a set of process improvement techniques and rules) and the Project Management Institute (PMI) recognize the role and recommend that projects have a project champion.

A smart project manager will become quite familiar with the project champion and solicit his or her advice in dealing with, and presenting to, senior management. The champion can then float ideas with senior executives, identifying and clearing potential objections and obstacles, before the project team recommends them.

A Mentor Advises a Person; a Champion Advises a Project

Mentor

A mentor is a senior and respected expert in one or more areas of the organization. He or she is knowledgeable, not just in the official procedures and processes of the organization, but also in the culture and unofficial—unwritten—rules of corporate engagement.

The mentor should be senior to the mentee by one or two levels and be willing to informally advise the mentee on his or her job, career, and path for success in the organization.

There should be no line responsibility between mentor and mentee. Rather the relationship is informal and advisory. The objective is not to have a buddy—that's what lunch rooms are for—rather, the objective is to have someone who can unofficially advise the mentee on when he or she is doing something right and when his or her is on the wrong track. Mentors are not a cheerleading squad—call mom if constant encouragement is needed—they are there to listen to mentee questions and provide factual and practical advice. They are not there to intervene with the mentee's managers to "fix things." A good mentor will resist talking to the mentee's boss if at all possible to avoid interfering in the employee-manager relationship or second guessing management decisions.

Everyone in an organization should have a mentor. Some organization's assign an official mentor; others allow employees to pick their own. Even if there are official mentors, almost everyone should also have one or more unofficial mentors.

Champion

The project champion is a senior member of the organization who takes a personal interest in the project. He or she regularly attends or is at least a guest at the highest level corporate governance meetings. The champion works closely with the highest levels in the organization (and is often their peer) and can represent and advocate for the project with senior executives. The champion often has the power to influence, if not modify, budgets and project plans, and commit organizational resources. The champion can often speak for the organization at project meetings and reviews.

Using the Project Champion

A good project champion can support a project in at least four ways.

Represent the project at the highest corporate levels. As a member of the inner circle, the champion can either advocate for the project (budget, schedules, resources, etc.) at executive decision-making meetings or make the decisions unilaterally.

Can commit corporate resources. The champion can directly make, or as an executive conduit, influence organizational binding resource decisions.

Keep the firm focused on the endgame. If the champion is sufficiently senior in the organization then he or she can cut through corporate red tape, thwart naysayer interference, and clear organizational obstacles.

Clear the decks for the project. The champion is not a member of the project team but rather an important resource to allow the team to do its job. Like a snowplow on a train, the champion clears the way for those who follow behind.

Project Champion: A Resource, Not a Buddy

Every project manager needs to remember that the project champion represents the organization and the project and not the project manager. For example, a champion might decide that the current project manager is the wrong person to lead the project and needs to be replaced. Both the champion and the project manager need to jointly understand the champions goals and responsibilities.

THE TAKEAWAY

- A project champion should be part of any systems development effort that is expensive, user focused, and business significant.
- A project champion is a senior member of the organization who takes a personal interest in the project. The champion can speak for the organization at project meetings and reviews and has the power to influence, if not modify, budgets and project plans, and commit organizational resources.

Chapter 9

Not Taking Advantage of the Honeymoon Period
or
What to Do on Your Honeymoon

Wherever a man neglects to take advantage of any defense
which he has at the time, he waives it.
~ Sir Francis Buller

The project is approved and funded and the kickoff meeting was a huge success. Project team members, IT management, users, and user management attended the project kickoff gala, toasting each other with their new project coffee cups and are almost giddy with anticipation of the new system scheduled for completion 18 months from now.

Six months into the project, the team is on schedule and on budget. Everything is going as planned. Project team morale couldn't be better. Yet, unknown to the team, problems are brewing that cannot only sink the on-time and on-budget project, but these problems might have been stewing since before the kickoff meeting.

THE PROBLEM

How could there be a problem with an on-time on-budget project? There are two major forces at work to bring a healthy project to its knees: the mid-project blues and naysayers.

Mid-Project Blues

The project plan says that the first user deliverable will be available in 12 months. The users agreed to the schedule and signed off on the plan, yet just a few months into the project, the user is getting antsy, nervously asking at every meeting where things are. The project manager's bar charts and progress reviews, showing that everything is copacetic, do not seem to satisfy user management. What is the problem?

The problem is the *mid-project blues*, the unjustifiable yet very real feeling that things are not happening as they should. The queasy feeling is caused by the amount of time between project kickoff and the first user deliverable—the so called, *deliverable desert*. It does not matter that the project plan says that the user will not see any user-discernable progress until month 12. The time between month 1 and month 12, which seemed so short on the bar chart, now appears as a vast desert with nothing to show for the work done and the dollars spent.

Look at the situation from the perspective of the otherwise support-ive senior business managers. IT tells them that the project will pro-vide the business with some needed functionality but that it costs X dollars and takes 18 months. Most senior business managers could not tell a mainframe from a refrigerator, even if they opened the door and saw the light go on, so they are taking on faith the costs and told to them by a seemingly exclusive and secretive priesthood that mumbles in a language that is barely understanda-ble by the common man. Even so, they sign up because, after all, what else can they do?

Everyone at the kickoff meeting was optimistic but now "reality" starts to set in. First, month after month, senior business manage-ment has to write checks to IT for unproven progress. Oh, IT says everything is going fine, but how does the business really know the truth? They are aware that they have no facts to support their con-cerns other than an uncomfortable nagging feeling that will not go away.

The Naysayers

The second problem is more real and more insidious than the blues. It involves people out to "get" the project.

Some projects are popular with everyone and there's universal agreement on the course of action. However, many more projects, particularly large and/or business-critical ones, are embroiled in senior management disagreements and intrigue long before any project team is staffed. Some senior managers might disagree with the scope, objectives, or size of the project. Others might think it should be outsourced. Still others might think it should not be un-dertaken at all.

Why? There can be genuine disagreement on the right course of ac-tion, or belief that the money could be better spent elsewhere (per-haps on their project), or simple politics (one senior manager not wanting another one to have a business success). For whatever reason, there are those who object to the project's timing, or its cost, or its very existence.

If the project was funded and kicked-off, then the dissidents obviously lost the battle—but the war might not be over. Many one-time project objectors become current project naysayers, taking every opportunity to point out project flaws or mistakes—real or imagined.

As mentioned in Chapter 8 No Project Champion, naysayers, at least the smart ones, do not bad mouth a project right away. The euphoria right after kickoff would drown out any negative comments and possibly even label the naysayer a…well, naysayer. The smart naysayer, the nattering nabobs of negativity (look it up), will even accept the project and wish it well, at least, until the time is right.

Then, after a few months, these same senior business managers—who opposed the project to begin with—now tell the project supporters that everything is not going as IT reports. They forward newspaper articles regarding catastrophically failed projects that sunk entire companies. Everyone knows someone, who knows someone, who lived through an IT project horror story.

You cannot hear bad news, day after day, writing check after check, with little to no impact. The doubts start to set in. This malady is similar to the *mid-project blues* mentioned above, only worse. Naysayers latch onto the normal *mid-project blues* and expand on them, elevating the once stone-in-the-shoe to a full-blown ulcer.

The Unfortunate Result

At some point, senior business management will call for a special progress review to understand "what is really going on."

What went wrong? The problem is that awkward time after the kickoff euphoria has worn off and the end looks so very far away. Every project has a *honeymoon period* lasting from the start of the project and continuing for a few weeks or months. During the honeymoon period the project is running on the goodwill created during its kickoff, with support high and criticism low. However, when the honeymoon is over, the project becomes fair game for valid as well as undeserved criticism.

How long is the honeymoon? Difficult to say. Every project, every organization, and its people and culture are different. It is the equivalent of an organizational span-of-attention, so the cause is more psychological than objective. However, a good out-of-the-hat number would be 6 months. For example, if you are managing an 18-month project, then you have 6 months to produce work that will impress friendly senior managers, placate those on the fence, and thwart the project unfriendly.

If your project is as pristine as the driven snow, then you probably have no worries. However, if your project is like most projects—bumpy start, some progress, some problems—it might no longer look like a bargain to the non-professional. Add in the naysayers and the result can be cancellation of a project that was essentially on track.

WHAT YOU CAN DO

What's a project manager to do? There is plenty. The project manager has the honeymoon period to ensure that the project and the team stay in the user's favor.

Meet Often With Stakeholders

Meet with project stakeholders (senior and business unit management) often—more often than you probably want to. One of the reasons once faithful senior managers go apostate is that the naysayers have been whispering in their ears. No one chucks a perfectly good project out the window after hearing a single gossipy tale of doom. Rejecting a belief requires a broken record of almost daily catastrophic predictions. Hearing relentless bad news prophecies can instill doubt in even the most ardent zealot.

The only effective remedy for this onslaught of fake news is to meet with project *stakeholders* as often as possible. Because the project manager might not have access to the stakeholder's other ear, then he or she needs the help of the project champion (if there is one) who might be able to cozy up to the affected skeptic. (See Chapter 8 No Project Champion.) The alternative is a number of short (very short) meetings (weekly if possible or whatever the stakeholders can tolerate) to keep stakeholders informed of progress. Demos are a great idea because seeing something happen on a screen is more convincing that a PowerPoint pie chart. User staff, particularly those assigned to the project, can be a godsend. Some IT geek saying everything is fine does not have near the impact of a user saying everything is fine. Getting the user customer service supervisor to report on how well things are going carries far more weight that a Java programmer.

Communicate Using Business Terminology—Not IT-Speak

Nothing can cause eyes to glaze over faster than a PowerPoint presentation on agile development. Consider your audience. They are more comfortable talking about depreciation than IPV6. Use the business staff assigned to the project for more than data-flow diagrams. Get them to spill their vocabulary and how they would report progress. Consider having the user team members present the progress report. Nothing says that the users are on board with the project more than having them telling their senior management how well things are going.

Because of training, jargon, and even turnover, some business people feel that IT staff work more for the tech industry than they do for the company. Business terminology (both general business terms as well as company-specific business jargon) does more than communicate. It also tells the stakeholders that the IT staff are onboard, that they are part of the corporate team. Nothing says that we are one of you more than speaking your language.

Gain a Reputation for Telling the Truth—The Good, The Bad, and The Ugly

Putting a positive spin on bad information sounds like a good idea, but it can come back to haunt you. Every project has glitches, potholes, and rough spots. Let's face it, if managing a project were a cakewalk, then an experienced systems developer would not be needed to lead it. It is not surprising that project managers try to protect their users from the vicissitudes of a normal project. Unfortunately, it takes only one instance of protecting the user, that subsequently blows up into a major brouhaha, to have business users question the veracity of the project manager. Remember users are suspicious of IT in the first place with its high costs, strange language, and sometimes weird people (their view not mine...entirely). Add in any notion of a lack of candor on IT's part and the naysayers might as well go home, their job is done.

The safest way to weather bad or questionable news is to have a reputation for scrupulous honesty. And your mother would be so proud.

Provide User Functionality Before the End of the Honeymoon Period and Every 6 Months Or So Thereafter—No Infrastructure Phases

One of the realities of many projects is that before any user functionality can be coded, certain technologies and platforms need to be in place. Hardware might have to be purchased, installed, and tested. The same is true for system software such as operating systems, network software, and database management systems. Development tools might have to be purchased and installed and staff trained before any application software can be written. Much has to happen before anything user-recognizable is produced. For this reason, for many projects, the first project phase is an infrastructure or housekeeping phase.

If the users are patient, and if they understand and believe in the project plan, then all is well. They will continue writing those checks and approving progress while the infrastructure is put in place. However, if they are antsy ("are we there yet?"), if there are vocal critics, if bills keep mounting and progress is illusive, then they might start to question the very plan they approved just a few months ago.

The only real solution to this very real problem is to ensure that the user sees business functionality before the end of the honeymoon period. Iterative and incremental project development methods (such as rapid application development, prototyping, extreme programming, and agile development, among a plethora of others) can help. Having a user ride shotgun next to a programmer/analyst developing a user interface can not only provide useful design input but also create a convert willing to extol to their management the value of the project. In the end, it is a simple case of use it (the honeymoon period) or lose it (the entire project).

The first three suggestions (frequent meetings, good communication, and tell the truth) are cheap and easy to implement; they just require the will to undertake them. However, the fourth, moving up user benefits to within the honeymoon period, is not. In fact, it is one of the most difficult and disruptive project planning tasks any manager will have to oversee. But it has to be done.

The Silver Lining

There is a development team benefit to pushing user functionality into the honeymoon period. Sometimes the development approach taken by the team has serious flaws. Discovering in month 17 of an 18-month project that the design approach will not work is not only embarrassing but career shortening. Discovering the same problem in month 6 might be embarrassing but probably well within the window to fix the error and still have a successful project (and career).

Will moving up user benefits to within the honeymoon period cost more and take longer? It might very well. But the extra cost of delaying infrastructure (if there is any) and moving user functionality forward, should be viewed as an insurance premium for increasing the odds of viable project results.

Too many project managers will see a chapter about the honeymoon period as a negative—you can't have an infrastructure phase, you must produce end-user value during the first few months, you need to converse with stakeholders, etc. However, a wiser way to look at it is as an opportunity. The team has the opportunity, within the first few months of the project, to demonstrate to the users that: (1) the project is on track (the visceral or emotional value of seeing something work is far more powerful than numbers or bar charts); (2) they made the right decision to fund the project; and (3) the current team comprises the right people to build the application.

This more positive and adaptive approach to the honeymoon period is also consistent with the ongoing need to continually sell the project to management. (See Chapter 14 Not Recognizing that Half of Managing is Selling.)

There Is Nothing More Expensive Than a Cancelled Project

Structuring a project plan that will provide upfront user benefit might not only require more think time but it could be expensive as well. Moving some functionality forward and postponing some infrastructure tasks can extend schedules and require additional funds. However, in most every case, it is worth it. Cancelling a project incurs costs and provides zero benefits. It is for the users' benefit that committed projects are completed and needed functionality delivered. If ensuring that every phase, or every 6 months, the users get something for their trust and their money, then that that is a good bargain.

THE TAKEAWAY

- The honeymoon period is the short period of time between project kickoff and when the project becomes fair game for second guessing the project. Honeymoon periods vary, based on corporate culture, internal politics, and the nature of the project, but an average length of time is about 6 months.

- An unscheduled, "special progress review," called by senior business management, is a sign that, in their eyes, all is not going well with the project.

- Avoid the dreaded special progress review by:
  — Meeting often, formally and informally, with stakeholders.
  — Having a reputation with senior business management of always telling the truth—the good, the bad, and the ugly.

- Regardless of the project plan, users need to see progress—a functioning system component providing or foretelling user benefits—by the end of the honeymoon period and every few months thereafter.

- The smart project manager will accept the honeymoon period and build the project plan to accommodate it:
  — User functionality within the first few months. Provide demos.
  — User functionality every few months thereafter. Provide demos.
  — No infrastructure only or other non-user functional phases.

PART THREE

MID-PROJECT

Chapter 10

Slippage
or
What to Do When Your Slip is Showing

The sooner you fall behind the more time you have to catch up.
~ Ogden's Law

Imagine you are running a 12-month, 60 person-month project. For simplicity, let's assume you are using a waterfall approach (makes the example easier to understand; however, the concepts are the same for any approach such as agile development) consisting of four phases (requirements, design, coding, and testing) each requiring 3 months and 15 person-months (Table 10.1).

PHASE	ORIGINAL PLAN-SCHEDULE (IN CALENDAR MONTHS)	ORIGINAL PLAN-EFFORT (IN PERSON-MONTHS)
Requirements	3	15
Design	3	15
Coding	3	15
Testing	3	15
TOTAL	12	60

Table 10.1 Original Project Plan

Assume that at the end of the first phase, you are three-quarters of a month behind schedule. The plan was to expend 15 person-months in the first phase, but you have actually expended 18.75 person-months, a 25 percent *slippage*—what should have taken 3 calendar months has taken 3.75 months. You have a presentation you must give to management on the status of the project. What should you do?

THE PROBLEM

There are four potential project manager responses.

Response 1. Lie. Well, if you are like many project managers you say everything is fine. You do this because you are convinced that you can make up the time (after all, the problem was a slow staff ramp-up, yada, yada, yada) and there is no need to unnecessarily concern senior managers who might blow the problem out of proportion.

Response 2. 'Fess up and Add the Three-Quarters of a Month to the Schedule. A smaller group will tell the truth and add the three-quarters of month to the schedule now making the project schedule 12.75 months with the effort of 63.75 person-months (Table 10.2).

PHASE	ORIGINAL PLAN		REVISED PLAN	
	SCHEDULE (CALENDAR MONTHS)	EFFORT (PERSON-MONTHS)	SCHEDULE (CALENDAR MONTHS)	EFFORT (PERSON-MONTHS)
Requirements	3	15	3.75	18.75
Design	3	15	3	15
Coding	3	15	3	15
Testing	3	15	3	15
TOTAL	12	60	12.75	63.75

Table 10.2 Revised Project Plan

Both are common answers, and both are a mistake.

Response 3. Adjust the entire project by the slippage. Go back to the planning process and the onerous job of estimating the effort needed to complete the project (see Chapter 5 Planning for The Perfect). Estimating is a bear and to a great extent (a greater extent than either IT or the users are often willing to admit), an educated guess. Effort estimates are frequently wrong, if by wrong you mean the planned and actual effort expended do not agree. (Rather than "wrong" I prefer to think of them as "dispiritedly different.")

However, simply adding the lost time back into the plan, as was done in Response 2, is not the answer. As mentioned in Chapter 12 Not Reading the Danger Signs, project managers need to ask themselves, what exactly is the project telling them and is it saying that there is a problem with the original estimating process. Ask yourself the following question, "If the first phase was off by 25 percent, then why should I not assume that each phase is off by 25 percent?" Maybe you underestimated the entire project by 25 percent. It makes sense. If the original plan called for X amount of effort for the four phases of the project, but X+Y was needed to complete the first phase, then why should one not assume that Y will also need to be added to the three remaining phases?

Don't like the old waterfall method (who does)? Then, take agile development's stories or any approach using use cases. If the first few stories or use cases take longer than anticipated to complete, then isn't it a safe bet that the remaining stories will also take longer to complete than planned?

Maybe the correct answer is to assume that you goofed by 25 percent and add that number to the entire project. You should report to senior management that you now believe that the project will take 15 months and cost 75 person-months (Table 10.3).

PHASE	ORIGINAL PLAN		REVISED PLAN	
	SCHEDULE (CALENDAR MONTHS)	EFFORT (PERSON-MONTHS)	SCHEDULE (CALENDAR MONTHS)	EFFORT (PERSON-MONTHS)
Requirements	3	15	3.75	18.75
Design	3	15	3.75	18.75
Coding	3	15	3.75	18.75
Testing	3	15	3.75	18.75
TOTAL	12	60	15	75

Table 10.3 Revised Project Plan

Is this a better answer than Response 2? Probably. If someone underestimates requirements by 25 present, then it is a good guess that the other phases will be affected. A 15-month project seems more likely at this point than the original 12-month one. However, while admitting that the requirements phase was underestimated by 25 percent is accurate, extending the rest of the project by the same amount still seems arbitrary.

There is a better solution.

Response 4. Adjust the affected phase by the slippage and then reassess the remaining phases. From Response 3 you know two things. First, you know that upstream effort is a useful indicator of downstream effort. If you were off on your estimate of the first few project tasks (phases, stories, use cases, etc.), then there is a good chance that the downstream tasks have also been misestimated. Second, unless you know exactly why the original estimate was wrong by Y amount, then simply adding Y to the downstream tasks is probably also wrong, because you have no real reason to assume that Y applies to those downstream tasks.

WHAT YOU CAN DO

What's a project manager to do? Take a mulligan. Unless you are a Russian roulette fan, anything less than revisiting the remaining project plan is a mistake. Yes, it's awkward, and you have some explaining to do to both IT and user management, but the pain now is minimal compared with the evisceration in store for you when the scheduled completion day arrives and the project is only half done. Bite the bullet and re-plan. It's what Charles Babbage would do.

Beware the Extraordinary Circumstances

You can almost hear it now. The project is behind plan but the cause was an exceptional problem that will not reoccur. The reason for the delay might be hardware that was not delivered on time or training that the vendor could not provide when needed. All of these could be an extraordinary one-time events that should not—will not—repeat themselves during the remainder of the project. Therefore, either Response 1 or Response 2 is an acceptable approach to the planning problem.

Maybe. Extraordinary one-time events are often…well…one-time. But beware. Nassim Taleb, in his book *The Black Swan: The Impact of the Highly Improbable,* points out that planners often reject one-time random events (black swans) as outliers that can be statistically ignored. However, he says that black swans are: (1) more frequent than acknowledged and (2) can lead to catastrophic results. The only way to deal with the random and unanticipated is to plan for them.

Yes, the hardware delivered late by a vendor might be an outlier scheduling problem not to be repeated in subsequent phases, but that does not mean that phases two through four will not have their own black swans. You simply do not know. The prudent project manager will look with suspicion at the claim of an extraordinary one-time event.

The Impermanence of Permanence

For its first large development project, a company in the Midwest enlarged the high-level project plan until it took up the entire wall of the corporate entrance area. Any changes to the plan would not only be embarrassing for the project manager but a blow to the corporation's self-image. Guess what happened?

There is an old military saying that no battle plan survives contact with the enemy—it becomes old the minute the first shot is fired. Project managers need to be aware that nothing happens as planned, and if the unplanned event is significant, then a re-plan is not only prudent but also required. Make sure that users' management is aware that the plan is more a living document, requiring constant update, than wallpaper.

THE TAKEAWAY

- Simply adding the amount of the actual slippage to the affected phase is insufficient.

- Simply adding the actual slippage to affected phase and the rate of slippage to the remaining work is probably insufficient.

- In most cases, the entire plan should be re-estimated.

Chapter 11

Scope Creep
or
Beware *The Creeping Terror*

Walking on water and developing software from a specification are easy if both are frozen.
~ Edward V. Berard

There is a movie called *The Creeping Terror* (1964), which is my pick for the worst movie ever made. In the movie, a monster—a carpet with a cloth horse head—shuffles up to its victims and swallows them whole through an opening in its throat. The problem is that the monster/carpet—propelled by three men crawling on their hands and knees under the rug—moves very slowly. In order to eat its prey, the victims must wait, with horror on their faces, while the carpet lumbers up to them at a speed a stoned koala could beat. Some actors even seem bored waiting for the monster to do its dastardly deed.

This chapter, however, is not about that terrible movie but something more heinous—*scope creep*. However, like the carpet...er, monster in the movie, its slowness masks its insidiousness.

Scope creep is the expansion of the effort or functionality of a project to accommodate new requirements after the project has started. This definition is accurate but misleading. Scope creep is not a problem if expanding the scope of a project includes the associated changes in effort, costs, and schedules to the project plan. If the plan is adequately adjusted, then the expansion might be annoying but rarely project crippling. What makes scope creep a pejorative term is that too often it does not include the necessary updates to the project plan.

THE PROBLEM

Practically everyone agrees that a major change to a project requires a re-plan (new effort, costs, and schedules) to accommodate the new requirements. What makes scope creep so dangerous is in instances where the requested/required changes are small. "Just add a bit here and a bit there and the user will be happy." A small change, in and of itself, will probably have little impact on the project. However, like grains of sand in a car's transmission, numerous and constant calls for small changes to a project can have a major negative impact leading both the car and the project to a breakdown. What sounds like a small problem is one of the great contributors to project failure.

Users are the primary cause of scope creep though it cannot happen without the complicity of IT and the project team.

User-Generated Scope Creep

It is a simple fact that the business changes over time, and some changes might occur after the project plan was completed. The following are common manifestations of user-generated scope creep.

New Requirements

The organization might acquire a new subsidiary that works differently than the parent and must be accommodated in the new system. Perhaps a subsidiary is sold off making some planned system functionality unnecessary. Competitor actions are often a cause for important business changes that cannot wait. Many of these mid-project changes need to be reflected in the final system.

Under Involvement

There is another cause of user-driven mid-project changes. Users, if left unattended, can downplay the required effort they will need to contribute to building a system. Business managers know that user involvement is necessary, but the number of their staff, their expertise, and the amount of time they will need to spend working with the project team is often a surprise. Once steadfast commitments by business management to provide functional experts to the team are challenged or given short shrift in terms when those experts will be available and for how long. User absence, such as an hour here and an hour there, might be small, but, those hours add up. Technical team members may attempt to fill in the gaps left by users, sometimes with unfortunate results because they often simply do not have the level of business knowledge necessary to build adequate applications. If user staff involvement is underestimated, if the wrong people are lent to the project team, or they are not available when needed, then incorrect decisions will be made. When these mistakes are finally uncovered, the team may need additional resources to fix the problems.

IT-Generated Scope Creep

IT is not immune to causing mid-project scope changes. Inadequate or poor requirements analysis can require unplanned rework as well as inadequately planned technology changes.

One problem that is often seen as a business-generated scope change but is really caused by IT is excessive *dream time*. *Dream time* is the time it takes for user articulated requirements to become a functioning and useful system. If dream time is short, then the user will have less time to dream up new requirements. However, the longer the dream time is, the longer the list of potential user change requests.

Every business changes. New customers, new products, new competitors, and new function and procedures have an impact on applications. They are simply unavoidable, but they can be minimized by just keeping dream time short.

Outside Organizations

Organizations outside the company can also drive scope creep. Vendors can cause project changes with new releases or versions of a product, withdrawal of products, or requirements for additional resources to support their products. New laws, government regulations, and even simple tax law changes can require system changes. Many, if not most, are unavoidable. All add up to doing more with the same staff in the same amount of time.

WHAT YOU CAN DO

Scope creep can usually be managed to be no more than an annoyance by employing some sound project management practices.

Robust Requirements Analysis

Many mid-project change requests could be avoided through thorough analysis of user requirements. Expanding the number of user interviews, ensuring that both junior and senior users are interviewed, and adding user functional reviews and walkthroughs can all but eliminate change requests caused by a mistaken understanding of current business practices. (You need to interview both senior and junior user staff. Business supervisors and managers are often only experts on the way things used to work. They may be unaware of low level changes made months, years, or even decades ago. It is often junior staff who know how it really works.)

Short Phases

Short project phases and / or using techniques such as iterative and incremental development (I-I) (see Chapter 5 Planning for The Perfect) can minimize the dream time window between user requirements and a working system and shorten the laundry list of changes users want to see.

Formal Change Control

Change control is a formal project management process that documents all user and IT requests for a change to an ongoing project; assesses the impact of the change, both benefits and costs; rates them on a formal scale, and presents them to a change control committee for disposition. The committee then decides whether the change is warranted and should be made now, is unwarranted and should be rejected, or warranted but should be not be implemented until a future time.

One could be cynical and say that nothing slows down requests for service more than a healthy layer of bureaucracy, but there is a place for a formal change control system. Put simply, a good change control process ensures that if the change is really needed, it is added to the project and if it is not, then it is formally postponed or rejected. Of significant importance is that a formal process gives the organization a way of ensuring that needed project additions are accompanied by their associated changes to the project plan.

The heart of a good change control process is the change rating system. The three categories (must have now; nice, but maybe later; and No) are simple enough, but how they are assigned is the crux of the system. The committee that adjudicates the requests needs to represent all constituencies and all management levels. It is important that those whose pet change is rejected feel that the process is fair.

Just Say, "No" (with apologies to the Former First Lady Nancy Reagan)

Not every organization has a formal change control process, and team-lead change control processes are not always respected by demanding users. If a project manager truly believes that a requested change is not in the best interests of the organization then someone has to say, "No." There are a few options.

Get Someone at a Higher Level to Intercede

This is an ideal job for the project champion (see Chapter 8 No Project Champion) who can turn a potential feud into a diplomatic success. If a project champion is unavailable, or unwilling, then IT management might be willing to take up the cause. Lastly, user management, more senior to the change requestor, might be willing to get involved; however, be prepared to find user management supporting user subordinates.

Just Do It (with all due deference to the Nike trademark)

Joseph Stalin is reported to have said, "It takes a brave man to be coward in the Red Army," referring to his orders to shoot any soldier who took a step back in battle. There comes a time when the project manager must make a decision. If there is no formal and organizationally respected change control process, and if no senior member of the organizations will step forward, then the project manager must either be the one willing to stand up and say the change can only be implemented with a re-plan, simply say, "No," to the change, or live with the consequences.

Scope creep is an avoidable project disease treatable by managing change requests and requiring that all accepted requests be accompanied by an associated review of the project plan.

THE TAKEAWAY

- Mid-project changes are an undesirable but often necessary part of systems development.

- Robust requirements definition will minimize the need for mid-project additions.

- Minimize *dream time*, the window between the business user articulating the requirement and the project team delivering it.

- Institute a formal change control process that—
    — Assesses the necessity of the change.
    — Calculates the adjustments needed to the project plan to make the change.
    — Decides whether the change should be made now, or made in a future release of the system, or not made at all.

- Just say no. Sometimes the project manager has to say that it is too late to make a certain change to the system.

Chapter 12

Not Reading the Danger Signs
or
Brace for Impact

What a sea
Of melting ice I walk on!
~ Philip Massinger

In January 1986 the space shuttle *Challenger* exploded less than 2 minutes after liftoff killing all onboard. What came out in the post-tragedy inquiries was that the disaster could have easily been avoided. All the danger signs were there and quite visible. They were just not acted upon.

The disaster was caused when O-rings, which seal the multiple booster components together, failed owing to the below freezing temperature at launch time. Protocols were not to launch below 39°F. Worse, some technical staff felt that launching below 54°F was problematic. In addition, on the morning of the launch, ice was observed on the spacecraft and surrounding launch facility. Add to this the partial failure of the O-rings in seven of the previous nine flights, and you have a recipe for disaster.

Technical staff voiced their concerns but were overridden by senior managers who either did not adequately listen to their own staff or were too afraid to intervene in so important an event. The result was the total destruction of the spacecraft and the death of seven astronauts.

Not seeing the warning signs and taking appropriate action is not an uncommon problem and certainly not unique to the space program. Many a disaster—as large as the shuttle explosion or as small as a cancelled IT project—can be avoided simply by looking for the signs, believing them, and then taking action.

THE PROBLEM

Ninety-five percent of all projects run into some trouble for one or more of the following reasons.

Over budget

In some organizations, the number one project *bête noire* is costing more than planned. In a world where money is king, mistreating it is a major character flaw.

Late

Delivering systems late is often the second most loathed project-related problem. Project lateness can play havoc with critical business plans and have a significant negative impact on corporate revenue (not to mention IT careers).

Poor Functionality

Software or hardware bugs, inconsistencies, performance problems, or ease-of-use issues can signal the demise of a project and/or its development team.

Wrong Functionality

It is amazing how many project teams simply do not listen to the user and thus do not provide needed functionality or provide it in the wrong sequence. Delivering the billing module before the order entry module might not only be useless to the business but signal that the development team does not understand what the company does for a living.

Loss of Management Support

Project teams need senior management support. Senior support is commonly understood to mean the user organization senior management and the project champion (see Chapter 8 No Project Champion). Losing one or both of these can result in questioning the need for either the project or the current development team.

Loss of Purpose

The system under development is simply no longer needed. For example, tax law changes could scuttle a new financial system (you do not need a depreciation system if company assets can be expensed) or building a multi-currency general ledger system just as the company announces the closure of its overseas operations, or a management decision to outsource the function.

Projects entangled with any of these problems can be candidates for substantial redefinition, downsizing, or even cancellation.

WHAT YOU CAN DO

The six problem areas above can be grouped into three broader problem categories.

Problem Category One: Team-Centric Problems and Solutions

This category includes problems and, in most cases, solutions that center on and/or around the project team. For example, budget and schedule problems can be objectively measured and the solution identified using a number of well-known project management techniques.

Budgeting and time issues are the meat and potatoes of most project management books. Although most do a decent job of describing how to measure budget and schedule variances, few of them are very useful in identifying what to do about them. Making the best of a bad Category One situation involves three activities: measurement, interpretation, and action.

Measurement

Measurement should be an easily solvable problem. The most junior project team members, back from their Intro Project Management course, will be awash in project measurement jargon. Soliloquies about cost variance, earned value, and work breakdown structure, by eager recently trained staff can provide more than enough numbers to describe the state of the project. In addition, most project management tools spit out pages of reports and graphs on project performance suitable for framing.

Interpretation

Now that you have the numbers, what are they telling you? This is not always so obvious. A zero cost variance, but a negative effort variance, could be telling you that a cost problem is brewing. Project managers need to understand the story these project management tools are telling them.

For example, measuring project management variances is a cookbook problem—follow the steps in the book or the software-package manual, and you will have all the numbers you want. What to do with them is more problematic, usually not in the book or the manual, and certainly not always obvious. If the project manager does not have the experience to understand the meaning of these numbers, then it is time to find someone who does; someone who has been a successful project manager for years and is willing to help the less experienced. This might be a good time to look for a (new/additional) mentor (see Chapter 8 No Project Champion). It might just be the smartest project management decision you will ever make.

Action

This is the task where the rubber meets the road. The numbers are there, and your brain has determined that the effort variance that will lead to a cost variance in the future is caused by the unavailability of needed technical staff. What do you do about it? The solution for many project managers is to do nothing. Like a deer caught in headlights, they are immobile. Many project managers are tigers when standing up to recalcitrant vendors but turn to pudding when dealing with internal management.

One of the biggest problems facing some project managers is not taking the wrong action, but not taking any action at all. As Woody Allen says, "80 percent of success is showing up." Eighty percent of project management success is doing what you know you have to do. If the numbers say that disaster is ahead, and you don't have any reasonable excuse to ignore the numbers, then taking any action is better than taking none. If you take no action, then the chance of failure is 100 percent. If you act the chance of failure is something less.

Without vigorous action, the measurement and interpretation tasks are a waste of time.

Problem Category Two: Team and User-Community Problems and Solutions

This category includes problems that are found within the project team but require the user community for either their detection or solution. Poor or wrong functionality can be difficult to detect, although there are remedies if the team is willing to look beyond technology.

Functionality problems—both missing and poorly constructed features—are the most serious user community problem. They often show up near the end of the project when budgets and resources are already under pressure. Remedying the situation involves three activities: measurement, interview relevant stakeholders, and action.

Measurement

Functionality assessments present an interesting challenge. There are really only two questions: were required functions developed and how good are they? Determining whether functions exist is rather easy; they are either there or not. The tasks associated with the features in question were either performed or not. The quality of the functions is more difficult to assess and will be discussed in the next step.

Interview Relevant Stakeholders

If you are trying to understand quality (or the lack of it), forget numbers. The best source for understanding quality is to interview people—in this case user staff assigned to the project, technical team members who have worked on the functions, and often user staff not assigned to the project but who have some connection with or vested interest in the system. If users have worked closely with technical staff in the design, coding, and unit testing of modules, then they can provide some useful input to the likely quality of the functions.

The goal of the interviews is to understand the features completed or in-process, how good they are, and what might be needed to make them better. Keep the interview positive—not assigning blame, but determining what has to happen to get the project back on track. Guilty staff can be ridiculed after the project.

Action

The goal is to fix what went wrong. If the missing or poorly executed features can wait for a future phase, so much the better. If not, then remediation might involve replanning the entire project and coming up with new cost and schedule estimates. Don't be shy about saying the project plan has to change. It's better to be chastened for something you did than something you didn't do (although perhaps only marginally better).

Problem Category Three: Team and Senior Management Problems and Solutions

This category involves the loss of senior management support or the loss of project purpose.

These problems usually encompass issues that are not easily detectible by the project team, require diplomatic skills unfamiliar to many in IT, and whose resolution is sometimes outside the scope and comfort zone of the project manager.

Sometimes a project loses senior management support (senior business executives or the project champion (see Chapter 8 No Project Champion)) or the project is now superfluous as a result of some senior management decision or action. In this situation, the project manager must decide to acquire new support, define a new purpose, or determine the best way to wind-down the current effort. The three needed steps are interview relevant stakeholders, gather relevant information, and action.

Interview Relevant Stakeholders

Loss of support. Loosing support means that either senior user management or the project champion no longer agrees with the need for the system or supports the manager or team developing it.

If the project is to survive then either new a senior user manager or a new champion needs to be found. This can be a dicey task because the relevant stakeholders sometimes live in rarified executive air. If the project champion is still on board but user management support is waning, then the champion should take the lead in bolstering user support. If the project champion is jumping ship, then either senior IT management or the project manager needs to find a new champion. If IT management wants to take the lead in finding a new champion, then the project manager needs to prepare IT management for the interviews. However, if the project manager is to lead the effort, then he or she will need to interview a number of senior business managers.

Be careful. Appearing to be questioning senior managers (versus interviewing them) can be more dangerous than dancing with elephants. Make sure all the senior managers you talk with understand that your concern is the project and project staff and that you are not sticking your nose in senior executive business.

Loss of purpose. Business reasons are usually behind a project no longer being needed. If the future of a project is in question, then a decision will be needed about what to do with the existing effort. Management could decide to redirect the project, repurpose it, or cancel it.

Gather Relevant Information

Regardless of who is taking the lead on communicating with top management, the project manager will need to provide input regarding the viability (costs and schedules) for redirecting, repurposing, or cancelling a project. The project team needs to play the supporting role of information provider. It is surprising how costly it can be to cancel a project.

Action

Every day that passes without executive support or a clear project purpose is expensive and makes the task of finding support or redirecting, repurposing, or cancelling the project that much harder and more expensive. The amount of new and unplanned work for any of these outcomes can be considerable.

What They All Have in Common

All three areas have a few things in common.

Measuring is often the major focus of the project management courses, books, consultants, and academic research and is the easiest task to complete. Software packages, project management cook books, and eager recently trained junior staff can provide almost any information required.

Interviewing relevant stakeholders requires not only interviewing skills but the vocabulary and confidence to hold one's own with senior staff.

Interpreting is where some project managers fall down. Numbers do not tell you what to do. Interview data can be deceptive. They can guide, suggest, and even point to the right direction, but they can also do the reverse. The good project manager needs to set aside the time to think through what all the data are telling him or her.

Acting is where most project managers fail. Head-in-the-sand is a very comfortable, and unfortunately, natural position. Having the right data and making the right decision, all comes to naught if the project manager fails to act.

Anecdotal information, gleaned from talking with project managers from all over the world, suggests that most project managers have all the information they need to make the right decisions. About half raise important project management issues with senior management. About half of those know what is the right thing to do. Slightly less act on that knowledge. Less than a quarter act in a timely manner. Why? Most hope that the problem will simply go away. Many are fearful of telling truth to those in power, while others lack the confidence to believe their own data and conclusions.

Remember, problems alone do not sink projects. Problems plus inaction do. Almost any action, if it is at least moderately reasonable, is better than no action.

THE TAKEAWAY

- If you feel that something is wrong, then assume that it is and investigate.

- Gather the data—from reporting systems, user interviews, and technical staff—and spend the time to interpret them.

- Inform senior management. If the problem is a lack of senior management support, then enlist help in either getting a new support structure or decide on the fate of the project.

- You weren't hired for your pretty face. If action needs to be taken, then take it—sooner rather than later.

- Remember, problems alone do not sink projects. Problems plus inaction do.

Chapter 13

What Do You Mean by Communicate?
or
What We've Got Here is Failure to Communicate
(From the Film, *Cool Hand Luke*)

The single biggest problem in communication is the illusion that it has taken place.
~ George Bernard Shaw

Project management tools are amazing. Not only can they tell you the status of your project, but they also produce numerous spiffy charts and colorful graphs that you can paste into the PowerPoint report you are preparing for that senior user management presentation you need to give. You are sure you will dazzle them with your RACI matrix (responsibility assignment matrix) and knock them off their feet with your Pareto Diagram (look it up).

Imagine your surprise when senior managers are not impressed. Hours spent color coding the work-breakdown structure wasted on an audience that does not appreciate the nuances of project management. To be fair, you might be bored at one of their presentations on RAROC (risk-adjusted return on capital), DSCR (debt service coverage ratio), or EBITDA (earnings before interest, taxes, depreciation, and amortization).

THE PROBLEM

The reality is that each specialty has its own language, methods, and measurements that are often understandable only to the properly initiated. It makes sense, you would not trust your favorite Japanese chef to fly your plane or the pilot to prepare your fugu dinner.

Worse, you might think that hearing all of that unintelligible-to-senior-user-management-geeky-jargon would make them realize that true IT experts are running their project. Not the case. You would probably be more effective reporting project progress through interpretative dance. Many senior managers consider jargon (at least not their jargon) a smokescreen hiding something you do not want them to know.

To effectively communicate, project managers need to see IT and the systems development process from the perspective of the user. Many users, including corporate senior management, do not understand what IT staff do and why they do what they do. They have a decent understanding of hardware—you need to buy it, you need to maintain it, you need to replace it. However, software and networks are seemingly unfathomable mysteries. You can see a computer; you can touch it; it has a physical presence, it is real. Software? It is intangible—who has ever seen it or touched it? It is not physical, so why do you need to fix something that is not physical—how can the non-physical break? Why does IT have people who dress like hippies (honest, who wears sandals in the winter?), smell like the homeless, (this is them talking, not me!), keep bizarre hours, and talk in a language unknown to anyone on this side of the Shire? And the costs! Why does something not real cost so much and take so long to develop?

They have a good point (except for the smell thing). They are competent and accomplished senior managers who know how to run their business. They might be experts in their respective fields, quoted in the *Wall Street Journal* or interviewed on CNBC. For them, IT is a very costly wizard shop of very expensive staff doing…who knows what. This uncertainty leads to many unanswered questions. Are the company's IT people "the good ones" or are they the dregs of the profession? Are they working hard or treating the job like summer vacation? Are all those dollars spent on things the company really needs, and what is the deal with the pizza delivery bills? They simply don't know.

It must be very uncomfortable for people who pride themselves on knowing exactly what is going on in their business to need IT to run critical parts of that business, to have it cost so much, to be overseen by such strange people, and to know so little about it.

Yet, the need is mutual and symbiotic. IT needs the business just as much, if not more, than the business needs IT. Organizations have survived without IT, but no IT shop can survive without an organization, behind it and willing to write all those checks. Therefore, it is incumbent on IT staff to adequately explain to business executives exactly why they are doing what they are doing, why it takes so long, and why it costs so much. IT staff who fail to learn this lesson might find themselves facing the Big-O (outsourcing), replacing them with consulting staff trained in business speak.

WHAT YOU CAN DO

If you, the project manager, can't present their RACI matrix and don't know what RAROC is, then you have to do something else. You have to ask yourself, what does senior management want to learn from a meeting with the development team? What is it that will make them come away feeling that those in charge of their project know what they are doing and are working in the best interests of the company?

Hundreds of projects, thousands of project status meetings, and more than enough experience doing the wrong things, has taught successful project managers that, when all the dust has settled, management wants to know three things. With apologies to Douglas Adams, we can call these the *Three Ultimate Questions*.

> **1. Is the project on schedule?** Will the project end when is supposed to end?
>
> **2. Is the project on budget?** Will the project cost what it was projected to cost?
>
> **3. Will it work?** Will the system do what it was promised to do—features and quality?

Anything else is either gilding the lily or obfuscation.

The challenge for the project manager is to adequately answer these three questions.

Less is More

Have you ever been to a really good PowerPoint presentation? Have you ever been to a really bad one? Content aside, one of the big differences between the good and the bad is the slide-to-minute ratio.

Bad presentations contain a large number of slides in a short period of time. If your 30-minute presentation contains thirty slides (slide-to-minute ratio of 1:1) then the odds are high that few people will come away with a good picture of the project and/or a good impression of the presenter. The truly good presenters have a higher than 1:5 slide-to-minute ratio. Why? Because bad presenters get it backwards. They think that the presentation is the slides while their comments are the background. The truth is just the opposite. The primary means of communication at the meeting is the presenter speaking. The slides just underscore some of what is said. The successful presenter, and the successful project manager, must hobble together, not a series of charts and graphs, but a story—a story of how the project is doing. People remember stories—nobody remembers graphs. There is no greater take-away from this section than...

> **Project Management Review Survival Technique One**: A good presentation contains a good story that the audience can take with them when they leave.

With this is mind, let's look at the three senior management questions.

Is the Project on Schedule?

Schedules are tricky. For senior management, some projects schedules are very important, while for others, they are the least important answers to the three senior management questions (cost, time, and functionality). The difference is when the system is needed and the impact it has on the organization. For example, The Hershey Company, the chocolate manufacturer, required that IT have its new business-critical systems installed before the busy Halloween and Christmas seasons (when most orders are placed). Project schedule slippage (read sidebar below) caused mountains of unfilled orders and put the very existence of the company is jeopardy.

The best advice for any meeting with senior management is to *know before you go*. If schedules are non-critical to the user, then the project manager of a late project will probably get a pass. If, on the other hand, they are critical to the business, then considerable pre-presentation preparation, including possibly replanning, is needed. If the project manager doesn't already know the importance of schedules to the user, the project champion (See Chapter 8 No Project Champion) probably does.

How Not to Do It

The Hershey Company undertook a major IT upgrade (installing packaged software for new ERP, supply chain management, and customer relationship management systems) in 1996. The original schedule called for a 48-month rollout but senior management demanded a 30-month rollout to avoid Y2K problems and be live before their most important business seasons (Halloween and Christmas) when they receive the majority of their orders.

Both schedule and feature problems made the implementation a disaster, costing the company a reported $100,000,000 in lost revenue. A good review of the disaster can be found at: https://www.pemeco.com/a-case-study-on-hersheys-erp-implementation-failure-the-importance-of-testing-and-scheduling/

If the project manager is unsure of the business users' tolerance for project lateness, then some pre-presentation homework is needed. The project manager should schedule interviews with a senior business manager or two to learn their allowance for lateness. Work on one or more possible solutions to the scheduling problem before the meeting—don't show up without some options for remediating the problem. However, don't postpone a meeting to avoid giving bad news. If there is bad news, it needs to come from the project manager and the sooner the better. Having management learn about it elsewhere can turn a bad situation into a disaster.

> **Project Management Review Survival Technique Two:** Do not present a problem without an accompanying well thought out solution.

This is a good place to learn a lesson from lawyers—no really. Every lawyer will tell you that they never ask a question of a witness in court when they do not already know the answer. They want no courtroom surprises. Likewise, a project manager should strive to have no surprises at a senior management presentation. Vet everything possible before the big event.

Is the Project on Budget?

Budgets can generate the most noise but are often the least critical of the three management questions. Budgets are what senior managers understand the best; after all, they have spent careers crafting them, enforcing them, and learning how to get around them. They can manipulate a budget faster than a politician can change positions. Their adherence to a budget can be fanatical while, at the same time, they can be eminently practical. If the project is needed for the business, i.e., if it will "kill more than it eats" (business speak for "generate more revenue than it costs"), then spending more than anticipated will be approved. Oh, there might be some public castigation of the project manager, but most of that will be for show. If the project is needed, then it will be funded. The project manager just has to utter some public *mea culpas,* and all will be right.

If the project is considered anywhere between unneeded and frivolous, then the situation is entirely different. An overbudget report is often the catalyst to kill the unwanted or undervalued. This is not an entirely bad situation. Cancelling unneeded projects frees up scarce resources for more valuable work. It can, however, be a blot on the project manager's career, though some perceptive and resourceful project managers have turned the tables to their advantage by being the one who recommends that, "for the good of the company," the project should be cancelled.

An awkward budget meeting can point out one important reality of senior management thinking. Both project management tools and project managers themselves tend to focus on actuals (schedule actuals, actual spend, tasks completed), while senior managers are more interested in projections (what will happen when and what will it cost?). Spend more resources and time on when things will happen rather than when things did happen, what costs are ahead rather than what was spent, and what features are being developed rather than what was developed. For example, if you are a nickel overbudget then you need to be prepared to explain the impact it will have on projected costs. (See Chapter 10 Slippage.)

> **Project Management Review Survival Technique Three:** Of necessity, project management reviews focus on the past (work accomplished, milestones achieved, spend so far), but what management really wants to know is the future (when will it finish?, what will it cost?, what am I getting when all is done?).

Just ensure that focusing on the future is not perceived by senior managers as masking past failures.

Will it Work?

This is by far the most important of the three senior management questions but often the least discussed at project review meetings (where the focus tends to be on numerical issued such as schedules and budgets) and the most difficult to answer for two reasons. First, there are so many questions to answer. Functional failure can be caused by a lack of analysis, or programing that does not adequately do what is needed, or the architecture cannot support the production environment (platform, data volume, transaction volume, etc.). The list goes on and on. When reporting on budget and schedule progress, the project manager has many numerical and presumably objective measures; however, there are few mathematical crutches when reporting on feature progress. Progress on the functionality landscape is highly subjective.

This is where iterative and incremental (I-I) development approaches, such as rapid application development, prototyping, extreme programming, and agile development, come into play. By having user staff intimately involved in the project, providing insight and reviewing work accomplished, senior business management has the input of their own staff regarding the progress and quality of the system so far. There is an added benefit. If user staff assigned to the project are excluded from the preparation and presentation of the project review, then they might take on a more adversarial position, searching for project flaws rather than extolling its virtues. On the other hand, if user staff are charged with reviewing and presenting functional progress at the management meeting, then their inclinations will be more toward supporting the project rather than criticizing it. Many a project manager has suffered a self-inflicted wound by minimizing the role of user project staff. The wise project manager uses business staff assigned to the project as ambassadors to the user community.

Lastly, do not stand up at a senior management meeting and toss a project management grenade—giving senior managers bad news cold. Short of announcing at a senior management project review that you won the lottery and are quitting your job immediately, surprises are not a good idea. Moderate less than good news is OK, but senior executives hearing for the first time that the project will not

119

deliver 50 percent of its promised functionality is not. Bad news, particularly about functionality, needs to be pre-sold, ideally with one-on-one meetings with selected senior managers. This is also the time to use your project champion (see Chapter 8 No Project Champion) to pour oil on the troubled waters. But do not dawdle. Bad news is like dead fish—it does not get better with age. Too many project managers procrastinate about giving bad news, but as awkward as it is for senior managers to hear about problems from the project manager, it is far worse if they hear about them first from someone else. Any credibility you had will be lost.

> **Project Management Review Survival Technique Four**: Never wait for a formal management meeting to present bad news. Always pre-sell bad news to the project champion or at least one or two senior managers before the meeting. No surprises.

Salty old project managers are awash with tales of presenting terrible news at a senior management meeting and getting no reaction, while getting skewered on something the project managers considered trivial. You never know what will pass without a sigh and what will cause a brouhaha. When in doubt, pre-sell.

Managing the Managers

Like it or not, a project manager needs to manage up as well as down. The project manager techniques that are so successful in managing subordinates are rarely the same techniques needed to manager superiors. Techniques and styles the work so well with programmers might be the absolute wrong thing to apply to user supervisors. The successful project manager has a separate tool kit for each constituency and the number one tool in the manage-up kit is communication and selling. A good project manager uses every opportunity in front of senior staff to sell they project, its benefits, its team, and its project manager. Anything else is shortchanging the project and the user.

THE TAKEAWAY

- Nothing makes a business manager's eyes glaze over faster than technical jargon.

- When all is said and done, senior business management wants to know three things (the *Three Ultimate Questions*).
  — Is the project on schedule?
  — Is the project on budget?
  — Will it work the way it was promised to work?

- Most project managers get slide presentations wrong.
  — They think that the presentation is the slides while their comments are the background.
  — The primary means of communication is the presenter speaking. The slides just underscore some of what is said.
  — The presentation should tell a story, with the charts and graphs only providing support.

- Project management review survival techniques:
  — One: A good presentation presents a story that the audience can take with them when they leave.
  — Two: Do not present a problem without an accompanying well thought out solution.
  — Three: Of necessity, project management reviews focus on the past (work accomplished, milestones achieved, spend so far), but what management really wants to know is the future (when will it finish, what will it cost, what am I getting when all is done?).
  — Four: Never wait for a formal management meeting to present bad news. Always pre-sell bad news to the project champion and/or one or two senior managers before the meeting. No Surprises.

Chapter 14

Not Recognizing That Half of Managing Is Selling
or
Do You Want Files With That?

Everyone lives by selling something.
~ Robert Louis Stevenson

Did you ever stay up late watching infomercials on TV? Remember that salesman selling that stainless-steel turnip slicer-yogurt steamer, "And if you act now…" He must have been talking more than 200 words a minute. Three a.m., a crummy set behind him, a questionable item that might fall apart faster than its overnight delivery, and it most likely made him a fortune. Why? Because, corny as it sounds, he was probably a good salesman.

Now imagine your best systems programmer in the same job. You might have the one programmer who would do it well, but many coders would have difficulty selling ice in the desert. What's worse, they would be miserable doing it. Why? Salespeople have a very specific set of skills. First, they enjoy meeting new people and are comfortable with them right away. At a party, they walk right up to people they don't know, introduce themselves, and start a conversation. Second, they believe in what they do. Take the car salesman who used to sell Fords but now sells Chevys. When he sold Fords he told potential customers that Fords were the best cars around. Now he says the best cars are Chevys. Is he lying? Maybe, but actually many sales people really believe what they say. They can change sides (Ford to Chevy) and truly believe the line they are feeding their new customers. They possess a skill (or gene, or disease) that avoids cognitive dissonance.

Sales people are going to hate me for saying this, but the ideal salesmen and saleswomen are politicians. They might deny it, but politicians are in the business not to make laws but to raise money so they can run for office. It's the campaign they love—meeting new people and telling potential constituents what they want to hear. They love the attention.

IT people, at least for the most part, do not have these skills or needs. Many in IT (and I know I'm going to take a lot of flak for this) are shy and avoid meeting new people. They are the wallflowers at New Year's Eve parties (assuming they were invited in the first place). And they like it that way. They know that they would rather stand to the side and watch the interactors than be at the center of them.

Too general a comment? Agreed. Customer service engineers and business analysts might do a somewhat better job of interacting with users than systems programmers. They also might enjoy it more. They might even seem socially indistinguishable from HR employees. However, while there are major exceptions, I think most will agree that we in IT, for the most part, are more socially reserved than a casket salesman.

THE PROBLEM

That was not the bad news. Here is the bad news. All managers—business, IT, and project—if they are to be successful, are salespeople. If you are a project manager, then one of your jobs is to sell your project. The initial proposal meeting—it's a selling situation. The kickoff meeting—it's a selling situation. The progress review—it's a selling situation.

And what about the senior business executives or user managers? They are salespeople as well. Many of them were *bona fide* salespeople. The others, based on their rise in the organization, have obviously demonstrated successful selling techniques.

WHAT YOU CAN DO

So, what's a reserved project manager to do?

Sell is a verb. The associated noun is *client* (or *customer*) or *stakeholder*, the object of all that selling. The successful salesperson needs to know a lot about the client, which, it turns out, is the first of six tasks the salesperson/project manager needs to perform. (Note: *stakeholder* and *client* will be used interchangeably to be consistent with most project management techniques and tools.)

Understand the Client

To successfully sell the project, managers need to know what the client is likely to buy.

Identify the Clients and Stakeholders

For the average project, IT's clients are certainly business user management and IT management, although clients can include others, such as employees (for a payroll system) the government (tax systems), and external customers (customer service).

Who Are the Project Stakeholders?

There is an old tale about the pet supply company that introduced a new premium dog food. Despite its upscale image, sales were miserable, so the company hired a topnotch marketing consultant to help them. The company executives explained to the consultant that they conducted an extensive advertising campaign, ran nationwide store promotions, and even went as far as to gain celebrity endorsements, but the dog food still did not sell. The consultant then asked a single question, "But do the dogs like it?" The stunned executives looked at one another for anyone who had an answer. None did.

There are many versions of this story, all of questionable veracity. Yet, within this tall tale is one of the most important lessons any manager can learn, "Who do I have to please?"

Not all stakeholders have a seat at the management table (for example, customer service reps), but they may have proxies, such as an employee union, whose interests need to be understood and represented.

Understand Client and Stakeholder Goals

Why is the user willing to spend good money on this project? Does the project need to be completed before a certain date (Christmas selling period for example)? There are issues that might not be publically known but that the project manager needs to know.

Know What Clients and Stakeholders Expect From Project Management

What do user and IT management expect from the project and the project manager? You would think this would be obvious, but you will be surprised to learn that user management, even IT management, can harbor strange expectations. Even though they all want a functional system, on time, and on budget, they might not all share the same priorities. User management might be most concerned with cost and least concerned with schedules, while IT management, mindful of its project backlog, is most concerned with schedules. Understanding stakeholders' priorities can be complicated and tricky.

Use the Project Champion

A project champion is a very senior executive who feels some ownership of a project (see Chapter 8 No Project Champion). The champion might hold an official position with name and job description in the project plan or charter or could be serving based on an informal arrangement solidified behind closed doors.

The champion often has the power to influence, if not modify, budgets and project plans and commit organizational resources. The champion works closely with the highest levels in the organization (and is often their peer) and can represent and advocate for the project with senior executives. The champion can often speak for the organization at project meetings and reviews. He or she either knows what the customers and stakeholders want or can gain that insight in the back halls of the organization. The project champion can function both as a project-friendly customer for the project manager and as an excellent salesman for the project.

Use Your Mentor

Every project manager should have one or more mentors (official or unofficial) who can help them navigate senior executive waters (see Chapter 8 No Project Champion). While senior executive mentors might be uninformed on the latest systems development techniques, they are probably pros on selling ideas to business managers and corporate executives.

Pre-Sell All Major Ideas

In a fair world, the project manager would be showered with accolades for successes and flogged for failures. Unfortunately, sometimes the stakeholders get it backward. The complexity of the project plan, arcane technology, and bizarre terminology can lead even the most fair minded executive to the wrong conclusion. Whether a project manager is to be praised or eviscerated at a review is not always obvious ahead of time. Sometimes a small incident or misunderstood progress is enough to land a project manager in hot water.

Pre-selling is having one or more informal one-on-one meetings, with one or more executives to discuss the meeting's topics before the formal review session. The purpose is threefold. First, the project manager wants to inform senior management of the issues to be discussed, ensure that they are understood, and correct any misconceptions before the formal meeting.

Second, the pre-selling meeting can be used to gauge senior management's reaction to the meeting issues. This gives the project manager a heads-up on whether executives are likely to be amiable, displeased, or even hostile to issues that are scheduled to be raised at the meeting. The project manager can then prepare a presentation targeted to the expected response.

A third advantage of pre-selling is the opportunity for the project manager to correct at least some issues upsetting to user management before the review meeting. Sometimes a quick fix can change a career-limiting situation into advancement.

Be Prepared

It is amazing how many project managers go into senior review meetings unprepared.

Formal Presentations

The formal project review is the primary venue for selling the project. (See Chapter 13 What Do You Mean by Communicate?) Many project managers go into a meeting thinking that the presentation is the slides and that they only provide background and commentary. They have it backward. The primary means of communication is the presenter speaking. The slides only provide background information and underscore some of what is said. The successful presentation is not defined by a series of charts and graphs, but rather by the story the presenter tells. (See the section "Less is More" in Chapter 13 What Do You Mean by Communicate?) The story includes what has been completed, what remains to be done, and any issues or implications going forward. It should be an informative sales pitch; not fluff and feathers, but hard facts that are relevant to the audience.

Informal Meetings

Every project manager should try to meet informally with every stakeholder. For some stakeholders, one or two meetings during the entire project are sufficient. Others might want the project manager to meet more frequently. Each stakeholder has his or her own interests and concerns and might even be disinterested to other project issues to the point of rudeness (talk bits and bauds to the CFO and the meeting might turn hostile).

Many project managers have less success with informal stakeholder meetings than with formal ones. The reason: lack of structure. Most formal meetings follow a formula: reserve a conference room, provide coffee and donuts, present a few PowerPoint slides, ask for questions, muddle through some answers, take the remaining donuts back for the support staff.

Informal meetings can be a minefield of misunderstood protocols, subtexts, and missed opportunities. There are, however, a few simple rules to avoid being thrown out of executive row.

Prepare to take the lead. A business unit president once complained that the project manager for an important project showed up at her office and apparently thought they were just going to chat. The project manager was told not to come back unless he had something specific and relevant to talk about.

The solution is to never show up empty handed. One project manager always prepared three PowerPoint pages of project issues he kept in his briefcase. If the stakeholder had some project issues she wanted to discuss, then the pages never left the briefcase. If the stakeholder had no project issues on her mind, then the project manager brought out the three pages.

Follow the top three/bottom three survival technique. Projects are often large and the interests of stakeholders can be arcane. It is easy for a project manager to get stuck with little to say on an important topic. You cannot prepare for everything, you cannot know everything, but you can cheat—well not cheat but rather improve your odds on not looking like an idiot.

Formal meetings tend to focus on facts: accomplishments to date, budget status, issues going forward. Informal meetings tend to be more question focused, with the client or stakeholder asking questions, sometimes at the prodding of the project manager. Questions might be about why the project manager is comfortable with progress or whether he or she needs more resources. Many executives want to ensure that their staff, the business experts associated the project, are providing what the team needs.

Being prepared for the *unpreparable* can be done if the project manager limits the subject to the *top three/bottom three* facts about the *Three Ultimate Questions.* (see Chapter 13 What Do You Mean by Communicate?) management wants to know most about a project.

- **Question 1. Is the project on schedule?** Will the project end when is it supposed to end? The project manager should know or have in her briefcase the *top three* things that need to happen for the project to finish on time and the *bottom three* (most probable) reasons it might not.

- **Question 2. Is the project on budget?** Will the project cost what it was projected to cost? The manager should have information on the top three examples of strict budget management as well as the (bottom three) cases of (real or potential) budget overrun.

- **Question 3. Will it work?** Will the system do what it was promised to do—features and quality? The project manager should be able to show or discuss three examples of functional success (top three) but also three cases (bottom three) of (real or potential) functional concerns.

Why should the project manager have examples of project failures in her briefcase ready to share with stakeholders? First, the client might already know. It is a common management technique to ask a subordinate questions when the superior already knows the answers in order to test the honesty of the subordinate—a powerful barometer of credibility and trust.

Second, it is better to get the bad news out in the open in a one-on-one meeting, where emotions can flair with minimal consequence, than in a more public venue. Both stakeholder and project manager have a more private setting to work out differences and resolve problems.

Why limit examples to the top three and bottom three? Would not the top five or bottom ten be better? The truth is the average project manager's mind can only hold so much. Knowing three facts shows that the project manager has some mastery of the subject. Knowing six would add little to the meeting while doubling the project manager's preparation work. And let's face it; absorbing more than three of anything is beyond the span of attention of most senior executives.

Manage Expectation

This sixth task—manage expectation—is perhaps the most important of the six and the one that comes the closest to encapsulating the other five.

An *expectation* is an anticipation or mental image of something that will happen sometime in the future. In systems development, users have an expectation of what the application they are paying for will do when installed. Of the three project planning variables (cost, time, and functionality (see Chapter 13 What Do You Mean by Communicate?)), the one that most commonly involves expectation problems is features. The user believes that the system will do X and instead it does Y. When systems development expectations get out of whack, it is usually not the one with the strange expectations who suffers the consequences, but IT.

Expectations commonly go awry for one of two reasons:

One: The user is unsure or unaware of the details. Confusion about what the system will actually do (its functionality) when complete.

and/or

Two: Expectations stray over time and can grow between their first inception and their reality. Like the guy who buys a Ford Focus, but by delivery time expects a BMW, there are senior executives who want to limit costs and development time during the project funding cycle but forget their frugality by project end. They are amazed to find that features, discarded as too costly during planning, are missing from the final system.

What's so insidious with this systems development disease is that the users are absolutely positive that they are right and that they told IT exactly what they wanted, and IT, owing to a tradition of underserving or some devious nature, has purposely ignored their requests and sabotaged the system.

If you have not experienced this, then you might find it hard to believe, but it is a real problem. Ask around. You will find someone in your organization who has experienced this horror show first hand.

There is a solution to this problem that is also the poster child for this chapter—manage expectation.

Managing expectation is the near continual, honest, and unvarnished feedback to the user regarding:

- What the system is supposed to do—its functionality.

  - During project planning, create a small summary document specifying what the system WILL and, more important, what it WILL NOT do. Make sure the user signs off on this document.
  - Keep this document in your briefcase and bring it to ALL meetings with the user, but only use it if you have to.

- Progress IT has made in building the system.

  - Make sure that progress reviews are user friendly and geared to the three issues that concern users (cost, time, and functionality).
  - Be honest—you're probably not a good enough liar to snow senior executives.

- What IT and the user need to do to successfully complete the project.

    — Lay out exactly what you will be doing between now and the next user meeting and any issues you think may arise.
    — If you need anything from the user (staff, cooperation, funds, etc.), this is the time to ask for it.

THE TAKEAWAY

- Recognize that all managers—business, IT, and project—if they are to be successful, are salespeople.

- The project manager needs to know who his clients are and what they expect for the project team.

- The key to selling success is constant communication with the user and managing their expectations.

- Managing expectation cannot be overemphasized. Without the constant feedback, expectations can go awry.

PART FOUR

ENDGAME

Chapter 15

Failing Testing by Passing on Testing
or
Testing Fails When Passed

Failure is not an option. It comes bundled with the software.
~Anonymous

Word association game: Pick the systems development word that is almost synonymous with cheating. The answer: Testing. Harsh? Maybe.

Testing is the most abused component of systems development. It not only suffers the most mistreatment but also involves a hefty dose of project management self-deception. It is a major source of angst for both the project team and the business user.

The project team faces three testing challenges: determining what types of tests to perform, defining when testing should end, and getting the user onboard.

Determining What Types of Tests to Perform

We all know about unit testing and functional testing, but have you heard of smoke testing or happy-path testing? Probably not. There is even a thing called monkey testing—it's out there—Google it. A short hop through the literature turns up literally dozens of different types of tests, some critical, some esoterically interesting, and some...well...downright strange. Some tests are encapsulated in other tests; for example, an online system GUI test could be a standalone test or part of unit testing, functional testing, or that favorite catchall, systems testing.

What types of testing the project manager should include in the project plan is largely determined by the type of system being developed. It's pretty obvious you don't need GUI testing for a batch application, but other types of testing are not as obvious. Should the project plan include scalability testing (testing the ability of the system's hardware, software, and network to support increases in user demand) or accessibility testing (the ability of the system to serve people with disabilities)?

Defining When Testing Should End

There are three popular ways to define when testing should end. The first is when a set of defined milestones is met. The second is when the number of detected defects (bugs) drops off. The third is when the system becomes useful for the users.

Ending Testing When a Set of Defined Milestones Is Met

The company might have a policy on when to end testing, or it might be specified in a project contract or the project plan. The key criterion could be meeting a specified schedule, exhausting the testing budget, processing a test file without any errors, or agreement by a panel of experts (technical and user) that testing is complete.

Most project plans spell out testing schedules and costs, but many go no further. If that is the case, then it is the schedule and/or the budget that determines when testing is complete—testing is over when the calendar says so or the money runs out. Schedule and funds are hard milestones that could bring testing to an end long before the system is ready for production.

Not nearly as harsh are more situational milestones, such as the system completes a test run with only X mistakes, or the user is able to process certain transactions error free.

Ending testing by milestone is popular because it makes test completion black and white with little middle ground. It is also, in the opinion of many experienced project managers, the least desirable approach to use.

Ending Testing When the Number of Software Defects Decreases

There is considerable literature on the subject of defect falloff. Some methods employ complex formulas and graphs, while others use simple arithmetic to tell you that the bug-finding corner has been turned. This method recognizes that not all software defects will be found; so the question becomes, not when is testing *complete*, but when is testing *sufficient*? Using these formulas, you plug in the testing numbers, and the result pops out—almost. There is still some human intervention required.

We should stop for a second and take an assessment breather. Testing is so full of unknowns that it makes sense to gather in one place what we do know. Regarding the question "when is testing complete?" we know—

> Reality 1: If the system crashes when running a test, then testing is not complete.
>
> Reality 2: If, for each test run, the number of defects uncovered does not decrease, then testing is not complete.
>
> Reality 3: If the number of defects decreases after each testing pass, then testing might be complete.
>
> Reality 4: If the number of defects is decreasing then testing is complete if the rate of decrease is *sufficient*.
>
> Reality 5: No one can give you a broadly accepted definition of *sufficient*.

So, there you have it. Using the software defect decrease method, testing is complete when, and if, the the bug falloff is *sufficient*. You just have to define *sufficient*. Remember Chapter 1 Not Defining Your Terms said that defining and obtaining agreement on terms is much easier before the project starts. If the project manager is on top of things, and read Chapter 1, then a definition of *sufficient* should be part of the project glossary and the project plan, on which the user signed off. When the bug count drops to *sufficient*, then testing is complete.

Ending Testing When the System Is Considered Useful for the User

A third way to determine when testing is complete is the system does not crash during testing, and the bugs still being uncovered do not weaken the benefit the business would gain from having the application in production. Another way of wording this is that testing is complete when: (1) the risk of serious system failure is deemed manageable, and (2) the business is better off with the system in production rather than allowing it to remain in testing. If these two conditions are met, then put it in production.

Getting the User Onboard

Testing can be complex and a mild mystery for the user. For many users discussing testing issues during the planning process is like discussing Easter decorations during Christmas week—perhaps important, but the timing is all wrong.

However, the user needs to be involved with decisions about the testing to be performed and even the definition of *sufficient* because they will eventually be called on to certify (accept) the system.

THE PROBLEM

The project manager faces three difficult testing-related problems. Two are self-inflicted and one involves user management.

Too Little Too Late

The project plan will include, not just a reference to testing, but also a huge block of time and dollars reserved for the activity. What too often is not included are specifics about what tests are to be performed and how.

It is amazing how often project managers sit down with team members just before the testing phase is to start and ask what type of testing they should perform. Half-way through the project is the wrong time to conclude that you grossly underestimated the time you need to adequately test the system.

Borrowing From Peter to Pay Paul

Guess how many project managers have cheated on testing? I don't know the answer either, but I bet it's a big number. Almost every project manager on the planet, at one time or another, surely has shaved a bit off testing to make up for some project slippage.

Why? Well watercooler analysis says that the number one cause is the project manager hasn't told the business user the whole truth about early development issues. Small setbacks, analysis or design errors, staffing or vendor problems, and recently increased knowledge of the system's functional requirements, can cause small schedule and budget slippages. Many project managers plan or just hope to make up the slippage in a future phase. As these small slippages add up, and as the project nears completion, the only recourse the project manager has, other than coming clean, is to reduce testing. Sometimes test plans are shaved, and sometimes they are gutted, but the results are often the same—the final product suffers.

What makes this situation even more bizarre is that the business users, who have been sticklers for following the plan until now, sometimes become complicit with the project manager and agree to shorten "unnecessary" testing.

System Certification—Where's That Bridge You Want Me to Buy?

There is a story about Christopher Columbus, perhaps true or perhaps not, and the indigenous people he encountered on his voyage to the new world. Columbus, a business man of questionable morals, craved riches from selling slaves in Europe. He had rounded up a number of natives to be sent back to Spain when he was stopped by a friar who told him that he could not enslave anyone who would convert to Christianity. Columbus, crafty devil that he was, then addressed the captives and, in Latin, asked all those who wanted to be baptized to step forward. None did. They were then quickly loaded on ships bound for Europe.

Although I question the veracity of the story, the situation is as interesting as it is horrifying. The captives were asked to make a decision couched in a language they did not understand.

For many business users, the language and functions of IT are confusing, but none more so than testing—yet we require their understanding and acceptance. We want them to sign off on testing plans, write checks, and then deem IT's job complete with little understanding of what they are getting into.

IT explains that testing is to find system defects so the application will work as planned. Then, just when the users finally start to understand that process and the costs of finding bugs, we tell them that not all bugs will be found and those found might not be removed.

If you ask a user, whether a clerk or an EVP, when a system should go in production they will say, "When all the bugs are removed." Telling them that not only will all the bugs not be removed but that there is computer code that will never be tested will seem unfathomable and indefensible to them. Why would you not test everything and why would you place a system that you know contains errors in production? Good questions. And what is IT's answer? Er…stumble…er…stumble, that's the way testing works.

Take a true life example. A company was developing a new customer management system. The effort had been underway for years with a number of starts and stops. IT, probably knowing a turkey when it saw one, turned system testing over to the business user. A marketing executive was put in charge of the testing effort leading a team of approximately 25 designers and programmers and 25 business users as subject experts and testers.

Testing did not go well. Many of the programs were in bad shape, some did not even compile. Months into the effort the error rate continued to rise with each test run. Staff became discouraged. The marketing executive AKA testing manager made two terrible mistakes. First, each test started with him publicly hoping that there would be fewer bugs uncovered in the new test run than in the last. When that didn't happen, he started to show displeasure with the errors and with the testers who uncovered them. The effect on the team members, particularly the business user staff, was as dramatic as it was catastrophic. The unintended and poorly hidden message was that finding errors was bad and not finding errors was good— the exact opposite of what you want a testing team to believe.

The second error the manager made was to start talking about summarily ending testing—because he saw it as useless—and to just put the application in production.

This is an extreme case, but the broader point is that testing is a rather complex and sometimes counter-intuitive process, yet one in which the user needs to play a significant role. IT is asking the user to be part of a confusing process and at some seemingly arbitrary point, signing off on testing and certifying that the system is ready for production—possibly with a hundred or more documented bugs awaiting a fix.

No reasonable person would pay the mechanic for fixing his car when critical parts of that vehicle are laid out on the garage floor. What reasonable person would accept a system with known defects and no plan to fix them before putting it in production?

WHAT YOU CAN DO

All is not lost, and the project manager can save testing if she or he acts before there is even a project plan.

Identify During the Project Planning Process All the Tests Likely to Be Needed

It is amazing how often project managers sit down with team members just before the testing phase is to start and ask what type of testing they should perform. Testing can be expensive and time consuming. It is not something that should be left to midway into the project. Test completion needs to be discussed and defined during planning.

The wise project manager will start with a list of possible tests and check off those that should be performed for the application—all before creating the project plan. As with other aspects of project planning, discussing and agreeing on completion criteria during planning removes most, if not all, of the emotional aspects that one finds during the testing phase.

Once the necessary tests are identified, then the implications of the list need to be considered. How many testers will be needed? What are the hardware, software, and test data implications of the tests? Will throwaway code be needed and how much (see Chapter 16 The Problem of Not Having Throwaway Code)? What resources will be needed to develop the necessary testing and conversion software? And so on.

Of particular importance is the discussion and agreement, by IT and the user, about determining when testing is complete. Whichever approach the team follows (milestone, defect rate reduction, or usability), it needs to be documented in detail in the project plan and noted, with appropriate explanations, in project schedules and budgets. The explanations are needed because no one—not the project team, not the project manager, not the users—really knows how long it will actually take to successfully complete testing. The only way to avoid, or at least minimize, business user pressure to end the project on schedule is the explanation of the vicissitudes and vagaries of testing laid out in the project plan.

The important takeaway is to determine what types of testing are needed before committing to, or even discussing with user or IT management, schedules or costs. It will be difficult to impossible to add an additional test once the plan is developed and the schedules and budget are written in end-user stone.

Don't Eviscerate Testing to Make Up Time

Testing is very, very important. Every experienced team member knows of situations where a system had major problems that were totally eliminated by a simple fix. On the other hand, many project managers have brought a system right to the finish line and then snatched defeat from the jaws of victory by not sufficiently testing the system.

It would be a grave mistake for the project manager to give in to the temptation to skimp on testing to meet plan. The relief of finishing a project on time and on budget is short lived compared with the subsequent years of living with an underperforming system. Listen to your better angels and work out a livable solution.

What can the project manager do when the choice is either complete testing and come in over budget; or skimp on testing, come in on budget, and hope nothing goes wrong? The answer is below.

'Fess Up

Do the right thing. Every team member is a professional and deserves to be proud of what he or she produces. If you need more time to do a proper testing job than own up to it. Tell business user management and IT management that more time is needed to complete testing. The average business application is in production for about 10 years. It's better to suffer some castigation for a few weeks than spend a decade supporting a turkey.

Explain, Over and Over Again if Necessary, the Critical Role of Testing to Users

Gerald Weinberg wrote a seminal IT book, *The Psychology of Computer Programming,* in which he looks at the world of programmers and programming. Weinberg delves into the heads of development team members and what he finds is often quite interesting and enlightening. His book is an important read for any IT professional, particularly managers.

An equally important book is *The Psychology of the Computer System User*, which devotes considerable space to identifying and discussing end-user testing assumptions, quirks, and fears. This book would help both project managers and development team members structure testing, as well as other activities, to maximize user understanding and support. However, you will not find this book on any IT bookshelf, because it does not exist. No one has written it; at least not yet. Without this important work, the project team has to plod along the best it can, explaining to users the mysteries of the testing process. And mysteries abound that need to be explained to the user community. One mystery is why not everything will be tested. The notion that there are too many things to test is a difficult concept to swallow. The second mystery is why not all bugs will be found and removed. Both seem to be such obvious necessities to the user that their denial seems like something out of Hogwarts.

The project manager needs to ensure every aspect of testing—what will be tested, how it will be tested, user involvement, when and how testing ends, etc.—is explained to, and understood by, the user before any contract is signed, project plan is attempted, or budget or schedules solidified. Of particular concern is the plan (budget and schedules). What the business users needs to understand is that, despite the team's best knowledge of the system and in spite of project management and systems development expertise, testing estimates of time and dollars are an educated guess. This is a very difficult message that many business users will question if not openly reject. The project champion (see Chapter 8 No Project Champion) could be of significant help in convincing the business user that IT is not trying to sell it a pig in a poke but rather applying sound systems development practices to the project. This is also an excellent example of the challenges of managing expectation (see Chapter 14 Not Recognizing that Half of Managing is Selling).

Oh, remember the company with the testing problem? It had the testing manager, AKA marketing executive, who discouraged finding bugs and wanted to put the system into production, as is, right away. Well, the company brought in a consultant to turn the problem around. The consultant, before even looking at the technical issues facing the team, started a reeducation program that would have impressed Chairman Mao.

Dealing with the second problem first, the consultant recognized that putting the system in production without further testing was a symptom of frustration, not rational thought. Things were so bad that the team manager thought why not just end it once and for all—sort of project suicide. The testing manager, AKA marketing executive, was instructed by the consultant to always have a positive demeanor about testing when dealing with staff, even if, after closing his office door, he curled up under his desk in the fetal position. Which, it is reported, he often did.

Need Help Explaining Testing to Users?

One of the great difficulties users have with IT is understanding that not only will every bug not be found during testing, but that not everything will be tested. They find it hard to believe that this lack of completeness is standard practice and not just the inadequacies or laziness of their IT staff.

Boris Beizer in his book *Software Testing Techniques,* points out an interesting fact that might help IT explain the realities of testing to users. He gives the example of a simple 10-character input string. This single 10-position field involves 2^{80} possible input and output streams. If you assume a computer automated testing system that can perform one million tests per second, then it will take twice the age of the universe to test all permutations.

To address the first problem, the consultant stopped all work, and team members were given a short course on testing philosophy that was long on discussions of goals (putting the best system in production) and team member success criteria (finding and eradicating bugs). Team building exercises (some that seemed silly but were actually quite effective) boosted morale. Unredeemable naysayers were executed...or reassigned.

Staff who discovered the most bugs were rewarded at team meetings with a close to ridiculous amount of fanfare and praise. Those who found the least bugs were encouraged to look closer and ensure that the code was bug free. Four months later, the system went into production and it worked.

The reality is that the entire systems development process can seem surreal for business staff. Testing—ironically the phase in which the user plays a significant part—can be the most confusing and counterintuitive. Praising people for finding bugs seems contradictory to the desired outcome only if you've forgotten that the desired outcome is a system that works.

Testing is the area where many of the remedies for other problems converge. Running a good testing process involves detailed estimating; early, complete, and descriptive planning; effective communication with users through the plan, project reviews, one-on-one meetings; and the project champion.

THE TAKEAWAY

- Include in the project plan a detailed definition and explanation of each test to be performed; the resources needed; and the criteria for its success, including needed testers (technical and business), hardware for the testers, test data generation, and any throwaway code needed to test or convert the system.

- Provide periodic and accurate testing progress reports to management (IT and user). 'Fess up when things are not going according to plan.

- Do not reduce or modify the testing plan to accommodate project financial or schedule slippage.

- Manage expectation. Explain, if necessary, over and over again, the value and realities of testing to users.
  - Estimating testing costs and schedules is an educated guess.
  - Ending testing should not be determined by schedules or budgets.
  - Testing might end with some known bugs not fixed.

Chapter 16

The Problem of Not Having Throwaway Code
And
The Problem of Throwing Away Your Throwaway Code

If it can't be reduced, reused, repaired, rebuilt,
refurbished, refinished, resold, recycled, or composted,
then it should be restricted, designed, or removed from production.
~ Pete Seeger

Want to quickly know how good a project manager is? Here is an old consultant's trick, ask a programmer on the team how much throwaway code was used during the last project. A good 80/20 rule is the more throwaway code in the system, the better the project manager. This "rule of thumb" is a rejection of the sophomoric notion that you are wasting your time if the code you write is not in the deliverable.

Throwaway code is the temporary software programs and routines created to help in the coding, testing, conversion, and implementation of the final (deliverable) system.

There is almost universal use of throwaway code in creating conversion software, the programs used to move data from the old system's files to the filing system used by the new system. After the conversion is successfully completed the conversion software is often discarded, leading to the label, *throwaway*.

Some developers use the phrase throwaway code synonymously with prototype or draft. They are talking about an early version or demo of the deliverable system. That is not what is meant here. An early version of a deliverable system is...well...an early version of the final system. Throwaway code, as used here, is the temporary code created to help develop the final system. Once the final system is delivered the throwaway code is dismantled and perhaps deleted.

Although conversion software might be the most obvious use of throwaway code, there are, in fact, many other examples. Programmers use throwaway code in unit testing to display application variables at different locations in the program. Database teams create one or more databases, long before the final database design is complete, to give application programmers access to the data they need to do their job. Throwaway code can also be used to link together programs to simulate an integrated system.

Some developers create entire test systems, occasionally rivaling the deliverable system in size. These test systems house test data in temporary test databases, run the test data against the deliverable system (the system to be tested), analyze and report on test results, and then refresh / reset the entire deliverable and test system so that the test can run again.

Throwaway Bamboo

Planning on constructing a 10-story building? Creating something that will stand more than 1,000 feet high requires a lot of temporary support. Scaffolding is one of the tools that helps construction workers safely perform their jobs. In Asia, the scaffolding material of choice is bamboo. Visit Hong Kong or Taipei or many other Asian cities, and you might find an emerging 50-story skyscraper encased in a matrix of 30-foot-long bamboo poles tied together with rope.

Bamboo scaffolding is both a science and an art going back 1,500 years. There is no lack of workers willing to do the job, with both wages and respect for the profession high. Yet, as soon as the building is complete, the scaffolding comes down with no trace of it having been there the next day. It is the installation art of the building trade.

Properly used, throwaway code is the building scaffolding of the software industry—an integral part of the development process with no sign of it having been there after implementation.

Near the end of the development cycle, a series of throwaway subsystems prepares the computer environment for the new system. Besides the conversion programs mentioned above, that extract data from the old system's files, clean it up, and convert it to the file format used by the new system; there are backout systems that, if the conversion from old system to new does not go well, removes the new system, replaces it with the old one, and applies to the old system any data activity (adds, modifies, and deletes) generated by the new system.

How much throwaway code is written for the average systems development project? Accurate numbers are hard to come by, but anecdotal information would indicate that in a few situations half of all code written during development is throwaway with 20—25 percent a viable average.

How important is throwaway code to systems development? Well consider that almost every commercially available development tool—from code generators, debuggers, and testing tools, to GUI generators, cross reverence tools, directories, and more— started out as someone's throwaway code. At some point, some smart entrepreneur thought there was an opportunity to share the best throwaway tools with the systems development community…for a price.

THE PROBLEM

However, there are two problems with the current approach to throwaway software. It is—

Too Tactical or *Ad Hoc* Given Its Potential Benefits

Throwaway code, with the possible exception of a conversion subsystem, is often considered the domain of the programmer. Individual programmers decide how much throwaway code they will create, when they will create it, and what it will look like. When they are done with it, if it is useful, they might keep it in a private library or folder; if it is only mediocre or worse, they might delete it.

Because of its low status, project managers have little interest in throwaway code's functionality or use. However, there are issues, considerably more strategic or project critical in nature, surrounding throwaway code that need to be considered. Two examples follow.

Example A: Finding Throwaway Opportunities — Backout Subsystem

Experienced project managers know one thing for certain, not everything goes according to plan. Stuff happens. Take this example: the conversion that looked so easy on paper turned out to be a nightmare. Worse, the severity of the problems was underestimated and was not fully recognized until the new system was in production for a week. Now the new system has to be taken out of service, and the old system reinstalled until the new system can be fixed.

This raises the very ugly question, did the team prepare a way to backout the new system and reinstall the old system without losing any data? In many cases the answer is "No." In spite of all the planning, few provisions are made for reversing the installation—that is, removing the new system and reinstalling the old one and transforming any data created, modified, or deleted by the new system into a format recognizable by the reinstalled old system, including all log files and journals.

Backout software, which can require considerable analysis, design, and coding effort, is not something most programmers would think of. (They would never consider the possibility that their code might not work as advertised.) This issue and the resources needed to address it reside solely with project, IT, and/or user management.

Example B: Finding Throwaway Opportunities — Reuse and Sharing

Throwaway code can be expensive because it is...well, thrown away. Sometimes that's fine because throwaway code is often poorly constructed, undocumented, and specifically geared to the application being built. Keeping it around might be a waste of space. However, there are times when the code written has value beyond its single use. Remember those entrepreneurs who turned throwaway code into Silicon Valley gold. They recognized that sometimes the one-time-use code has value beyond a single use and beyond a single organization.

The project manager is too often not aware of all the throwaway code used on a project and certainly, without a thorough examination, unaware of which routines are candidates for reuse.

Too Often Unplanned

Project managers work hard to ensure that all deliverables are considered when creating the project plan. To calculate costs and schedules with some hope of accuracy, the project manager needs to know exactly what will to be delivered to the user. As expressed in Chapter 5 Planning for The Perfect, this is a daunting task. Figuring out what has to be delivered, before what has to be delivered is defined, is difficult enough, but this is only the start of the project manager's headaches.

Throwaway Reuse

A project manager for a medium-sized systems development effort observed that one of her programmers used a simple function to aid in the unit testing of an online subsystem. The programmer created a small one-line module that displayed two numbers in the top right corner of the computer screen. The first, a two-digit number, was a *program number* created by the programmer and unique to each program, subroutine, or module. The second, a three-digit number, was a *sequence number* representing a location in the program. Every few lines of code and before and after every subroutine call, the programmer inserted the function with an incremented *sequence number*. If the program failed, then the screen would display the last *sequence number* where the program worked properly. The programmer then knew that the failure was after the last displayed *sequence number* but before the next *sequence number*. The programmer called his function *the mole* because a different *sequence number* popped up every microsecond or so. After the system passed all tests, all calls to *the mole* were removed with a simple program editor command or turned off through a parametric software switch.

The project manager was impressed with *the mole*, had all the programs and modules in the system issued unique *program numbers*, and instructed all of her programmers to use *the mole*. After the project was completed, she recommended to IT management that *the mole* to be used department wide, exhibiting a great example of throwaway code reuse.

Chapter 5 discussed a number of estimating techniques designed to help the project manager estimate the effort required to build the system. All of these techniques require some pre-estimate estimate or starting point called a *seed*. COCOMO requires the project manager to estimate the lines of code in the final system before an effort estimate can be calculated. Function point analysis requires a fairly decent estimate of the number of function points in the final system, while agile development requires an estimate of the number and size of the stories in the system to determine the seed. In all these examples, the lines of code, function points, stores, etc., are for the final delivered system. But what about throwaway code? Because throwaway code can be considerable in size, perhaps 25 percent of the total code written, it needs to be accounted for when developing the project plan.

Sometimes the project manager is astute enough to include conversion software in the seed. Rarely are any other forms of throwaway code, such as backout programs, included. The truth is that throwaway code is usually a planning afterthought.

WHAT YOU CAN DO

This is one of those cases where the recognition of the problem is three-quarters of the solution. If you discover that eating dirt is bad for you, then the solution is as simple as, "don't eat dirt." For the project manager, three-quarters of the solution is as simple as looking for opportunities to avoid throwaway code pitfalls. The two suggestions below will help.

Make Throwaway Code an Integral Part of the Project and Project Management

The project manager should consider the need, development, and use of all throwaway code as both an integral part of the system being developed and its potential for reuse.

Recognize Throwaway Code as a Project Management Tool

A famous French politician once said that war was too important to be left to the generals. Ignoring any potential wisdom that might be in that statement, it can be said with confidence that throwaway code is too important to be left to the programmers.

Its status needs to be raised from coding tool to potentially important subsystems requiring project manager, analyst, and designer attention.

Management can delegate unit testing to programmers, but major issues, such as conversion, system testing, and backout systems need to be given management attention.

Propagate Best Practices

Entrepreneurial wisdom can be applied to IT as well. Routines that were deemed throwaway should be examined for their potential future use. Reuse can be as simple as storing no longer needed code "as is" or generalizing routines for a more varied and general adoption. This approach is not new to software vendors, who view their internal software libraries of reusable code as a critical systems development advantage that provides a foundation for better and cheaper systems.

Any IT shop can do the same for little or no cost. It just requires the project manager, or someone delegated to the task, to visit the trenches in search of throwaway gems. Then project managers or IT needs to see that worthy routines are properly documented, housed, and their use encouraged.

Include Throwaway Code in the Planning Process

As shown above, throwaway code can be a considerable part of the overall systems development project. Up to half of the code written can be classified as throwaway involving person-months of analyst, designer, and programmer time. Yet, too often, it is underrepresented, if it is represented at all, in the project plan. Sometimes, even talking about throwaway code to user management is a non-starter. Business managers can find the notion that IT will be spending time, on their dime, doing work that will not be in their application as untenable. The project champion (see Chapter 8 No Project Champion) or IT management might be useful in defending to business management the use of such efforts. A better approach is to bundle the effort required to generate the necessary throwaway code in the project plan (see Chapter 1 Not Defining Your Terms).

Once again the pressure point is the project plan. Estimating the effort required to build an application is hard enough, but estimating the effort required to create an unknown amount of throwaway code is an order of magnitude harder (see Chapter 5 Planning for the Perfect).

A Useful Way to Look at Throwaway Code

A useful approach for explaining throwaway code to business management is to liken it to an insurance policy for which you pay a small premium to avoid large potential disasters. If all goes well, then the small premium cost might not have been needed, but it is good to know that there is some protection available even if the odds of needing it are small. It is simply a cost of doing business.

Project insurance issues are the domain of the project manager, who must determine where there is potential risk, if that risk should be mitigated, and what that mitigation might cost. Inexperienced project managers, oblivious to many risks, are not as inclined to take out an insurance policy. Experienced project managers know better.

The prudent project manager uses a broad array of inputs (team members, project management history, system complexity, to name a few) to understand the planning implications of creating and using assets, both delivered and undelivered to the user.

THE TAKEAWAY

- Throwaway code is the software written, not as part of the final deliverable, but as the support structure for the creation of the final deliverable.

- Throwaway code includes the software created for the coding, testing, conversion, and implementation of the final deliverable.

- Although it is usually considered the domain of the programmer, the project manager needs to be intimately involved in the creation, use, and reuse of throwaway code.

- The size and complexity of some throwaway code means that it needs to be included in the project planning process and its effort and time reflected in budgets and schedules.

- Not all throwaway code should be thrown away. Valuable routines should be supported and their reuse encouraged by IT management.

Chapter 17

No Post-Project Review
or
It's Not Over Till It's Over
(Yogi Berra)

Whoever wishes to foresee the future must consult the past;
for human events ever resemble those of preceding times.
~ Niccolo Machiavelli

If you are a gambler and someone offers you a bet on whether or not a certain project included a post-project review (PPR), take the bet. Very few projects include a formal and adequate post–project review (AKA post-implementation review). So why bother having a chapter with that title? Because hope springs eternal, and a PPR can be one of the best investments a project manager and an entire company can make.

THE PROBLEM

Take the example of a typical disconnect between the user and IT on forecasting project costs and schedules. IT organizations collectively have a history of coming in late and over budget. Being late and over budget might be understandable for an IT organization that develops few systems internally, but the forecasting problem also exists in shops that develop large numbers of applications. The culprit? The F word.

Multiple chapters of this book (Chapter 5 Planning for the Perfect, Chapter 10 Slippage, Chapter 11 Scope Creep, Chapter 12 Not Reading the Danger Signs, Chapter 13 What Do You Mean by Communicate?, and Chapter 14 Not Recognizing That Half of Managing Is Selling) deal with the problems of estimating effort, time, and cost, and the implications of those estimates. Although there are many estimating tools and techniques (See Chapter 5 Planning for the Perfect) they all require a starting point or seed. Where do the best seeds come from? Without a doubt, the best seeds, the best estimating processes start with the project manager's and IT's systems development history.

> Question: Want to understand how well project manager Mary Lou will do on this new project?
> Answer: Look at how well Mary Lou did on the last few projects she managed.

Project management history will not only give you a starting point for estimating the new project but it will tell you whether Mary Lou is improving as a project manager and perhaps capable of handling new challenges.

Most everything we do we get better at with practice. With sufficient practice, the 5-foot-6-inch basketball player can outperform the 6-foot Brobdingnagian every time. The key to practice is repetition—do the same thing over and over until it becomes ingrained in body and mind. However, repetition is a double-edged sword. Repeating the wrong thing over and over again habituates bad performance that can become enormously difficult to overcome. The special sauce in good practice, in good repetition, is the F word—feedback. Athletes need feedback so that they know exactly what they are doing right and what they are doing wrong. With feedback, they can modify routines, correct mistakes, and reinforce the right moves. A coach, observer, or a video showing the athletes performing, can provide the necessary feedback.

Project management is another of those areas where practice alone does not seem to improve performance—particularly in estimating effort, time, and cost. Many 50-year old project managers are no better now than they were at age 30. The project manager that performs the fifth time leading a project team no better than the first, second, or third time is intellectually stalled.

The solution is, once again, feedback. All project managers need to know their and their organizations' systems development history. The project's PPR is a chapter in the project manager's and IT's history book. It provides necessary feedback so that project managers can continually learn and improve project management skills. It can also play a valuable learning tool for other project managers, or would-be project managers, in what to do, what not to do, and what to avoid like the plague.

However, it can only do this if a robust and truthful PPR exists.

WHAT YOU CAN DO

The Internet is awash with PPR templates and sample reports free for downloading. You need only pick one and follow it. They all look a bit different, but the differences are largely unimportant if they include the seven sections listed below.

1. Closure—official end of the project. The section should include—
    A.   Project Summary. A few simple paragraphs that could be copied from the original project proposal. You might think this is unneeded (everyone knows what the project is about), but 5 years from now, these few paragraphs might be invaluable to a reader.
    B.   Project sponsors and champions.
    C.   Team members, both IT and user.
    D.   Project plan highlights—estimates of critical deliverables, dates, costs, etc.
    E.   Final Deliverables—a statement that the system was delivered and the project officially completed.

2. Goals.
    A.   Starting goals.
    B.   Goal changes during development.
    C.   Goals met (from the perspective of both the user and IT if there are any differences).
    D.   Goals not met (if any).
    E.   Plan to meet unmet goals (if any).

3. Major changes during development to—
    A.   Functionality (functions added, modified, and deleted).
    B.   Staffing.
    C.   Technology.
    D.   Project Plan (costs and schedules).

4. Recommendations for future management and support of the developed system.
        You might think that telling the user that maintenance is required on a system starting Day-1 is unnecessary, but it doesn't hurt to reinforce the message.

5. Final costs.
      A.   Planned costs.
      B.   Actual costs.
      C.   Explanations of discrepancies (if any).

6. Lessons Learned.
> This is a review of what worked, what didn't work, and why. This section is the lynchpin of any hope for future project managers to learn from the experiences of those who went before them. The project manager should detail what worked well, what could have been done differently, and exactly how it should have been done differently. All subjects are fair game including tools, techniques, staff (user and IT), productivity, user availability, testing issues, working conditions (office space, technical resources, pizza delivery, etc.), and even the moments of brilliance as well as the mistakes made by the project manager. It is essential that the review be honest and detailed.

7. Recommendations for future systems development efforts.
> This section is the logical follow-on to Section 6, Lessons Learned. Here the project manager is speaking to future project managers (or your future self), detailing what future project managers should look for, what they should avoid, and what to do in certain situations. Think of Dear Abby giving lovelorn advice, only here the advice is for future project managers.

There are a few critical success factors for a good PPR.

Bundle the PPR into the Project Plan

As stated above, having a robust post-project review, or any PPR at all, is unusual. The best way a project manager can increase the chances of a decent PPR is to bundle the review (including its schedules and costs) into the project plan. Get both IT and user management, if not on board, at least familiar with the PPR concept and budget implications right from the beginning. Make sure that the PPR is prominently presented at every project review meeting that discusses the project plan.

Having a prominent PPR in the project plan does not necessarily mean that all will go well. Down the project road, particularly if there are cost or schedule pressures, there might be a movement to drop or emasculate the PPR. If user management refuses to fund the PPR then the project manager should try to have IT foot the bill. The project champion might also be useful in convincing the user and IT of the importance of a robust PPR (see Chapter 8 No Project Champion). It might take some selling (see Chapter 14 Not Recognizing that Half of Managing is Selling) but if the project manager focuses on the benefits to IT, all might turn out well.

Positives and Negatives

This is not summer camp where every kid gets a trophy. Lay out what went well but also point out what could have been better. Do not defend what is not defensible. If IT management failed to have needed developers or development tools available on time, say it. If user management never provided the space the team needed and was promised, say it. It will not get better on its own.

Be Honest and Objective

There is no sense in going through the effort of a PPR if it becomes a puff piece (just the good things) or thin soup (a two-page Hallmark card congratulating the team). Remember all those times you went home and kicked the dog. This is the opportunity to explain those vet bills, bare the soul with the frustrations of being a systems developer, and help the next project's team members with better canine relationships. (Don't worry about retaliation. When was the last time user or IT management voluntarily read a project team deliverable?)

Honesty is particularly needed in understanding project productivity. Accounting can give you an accurate dollars spent (cost) on the project, and HR the staff hours consumed (effort), both of which might be the only numbers that senior management cares about. However, for understanding productivity, both of these numbers are useless without also considering the work completed (the fully developed and tested functionality in the system). If functions were eliminated or their usefulness reduced, if testing was abbreviated, and/or if documentation was shortchanged, and these changes are not taken into account when calculating productivity, then a false number will emerge. The cycle of poor and inaccurate feedback will continue, and any hope of project managers learning from their experiences will evaporate.

Many Inputs and Many Comments From Many People

The PPR is not the project manager's opportunity to settle scores. Every team member, IT and user, IT management and user management, should have the opportunity to add his or her comments and rants to the PPR. The PPR is not a social media blog. There should be an "official" opinion penned by the project manager; however, just as the U.S. Supreme Court might have a minority opinion accompanying the opinion of the majority, there should be an opportunity and place in the PPR for those who disagree with the project manager to post their opinion.

Done properly the post-project review can be one of the most useful and most cost-effective tools in IT's systems development arsenal.

THE TAKEAWAY

- Feedback—knowing how well past projects were executed—is critical if project manager skills are to grow with experience.

- The PPR needs accurate numbers regarding the costs, effort, and functionality delivered.

- The PPR needs to be a detailed and honest assessment of what went right in the project, what didn't, and what should have been done differently.

- The voices of all project stakeholders should be represented in the PPR.

PART FIVE

GILDING THE LILY

Chapter 18

And Now for Something Completely Different

No one is dumb who is curious.
The people who don't ask questions remain clueless throughout their lives.
~ Neil deGrasse Tyson

Vision without action is a daydream. Action without vision is a nightmare.
~ Japanese Proverb

So far this book has been—consistent with its chapter titles—quite negative: don't do X; don't do Y; whatever you do, don't do Z. Yes, being positive is out of character with the first 17 chapters. Positive things are often harder to accomplish because they can be expensive: hire the best people, buy the best equipment, provide the best training. However, there are a few positive things the project manager can do that cost nothing.

One positive recommendation to project managers is be smart—intelligent people do better in almost every job. However, because we don't control intelligence, we have to pass on this one. It might be good to be smart but what we have is what we have. It's like saying no one should be taller than necessary. Everyone knows it's true, but what are the awkwardly tall (guys over five foot eight and females over five feet) to do?

No, the positive advice needs to be actionable, meaning it is something the project manager, every project manager of every intelligence and height, can do. Below are a few things doable by even the tallest people.

Question, Question, Question

President Reagan was fond of saying, "Trust, but verify." The same is true for project management. Did the team really complete that last task? Is the pricing module really working? Did the pizza bill really break $100 last week? They say the devil is in the details. Wrong! Salvation is in the details, and that is where the project manager needs to be.

Just taking someone's word for it is a shining example of mediocrity, the home of the complacent and chronically underperforming. Every team member, from the programming genius who barely tolerates any form of management to the team neophyte, needs to feel that the project manager is on top of their work.

There are two big caveats to the above. First, there is a difference between taking an interest in team members' work and micromanaging. The former is asking to see what they are working on, and having them show you their progress, review their plans, and discuss their issues. The latter is an annoying intrusion of thinly veiled instructions on how to do what they probably know more about than you do. If you are not sure you know the difference, then you don't know the difference. Tread lightly.

The second caveat is that if you try to understand everything going on in detail in your project then you will burn out long before the project is over. (See Chapter 14 Not Recognizing That Half of Managing Is Selling for a discussion of the *top three/bottom three survival technique.*) Take a page from auditors who survey the subject they are auditing and then take a deep dive into every n-th one. Rather than a cursory look at everything, select a few samples and get into their shorts.

Questioning needs to be tied to a deep curiosity and a strong and healthy skepticism. This is not mistrust of the team members but rather fulfilling the project manager's job description—seeing first hand that project goals are being met, that the users' wishes are being carried out, and that the company's money is well spent.

A lot of work? Yes. If there is a patron saint for the project manager, it is probably Vishnu, the many-armed Hindu god, who, presumably, can have hands in many things simultaneously. The mantra should be, "Show me." Difficult? Yes. Doable? Yes. Necessary? Yes.

The end result of all this questioning, curiosity, and skepticism is one of the most potent weapons in a project manager's quiver, a defensible set of *project facts.*

Honesty

Chapter 9 Not Taking Advantage of the Honeymoon Period, Chapter 15 Failing on Testing by Passing on Testing, and Chapter 17 No

Post-Project Review talk about being honest with users and management, but before a project manager can be honest with constituents he or she has to be honest with him or herself. The amount of self-deception that can go on in a project is amazing. Like a deer caught in headlights, many project managers see danger and freeze. The desire to gloss over errors, to wait and see if things are really as bad as originally thought, or if they somehow autocorrect, is very strong, very natural, and very self-destructive. The more unnatural act is to address the problem as soon as it's discovered (didn't know you were being paid to perform unnatural acts did you?). Some team members might feel that "reporting every little thing wrong" is a betrayal of the team, the project, and IT. But this is where the rubber meets the road, the task that separates the men from the boys, is put up or shut up time, every good boy does fine, etc. It is the project manager's *raison d'être*.

Once project managers are brutally honest with themselves, they can turn their attention to reporting project status to user and IT management.

Honesty—Principle or Conclusion?

Let's clear up one point. The honesty mentioned in this book is not a *moral* principle.

What we are talking about is an expedient conclusion drawn from the experiences of successful project managers who have observed or learned the hard way that project manager honesty is the better and safer course of action. They would argue that even if you cheat on your taxes, lie on your resume, and create tall tales for your former classmates at your high school reunion, you should, for practical reasons, be honest with your project constituents. The vast majority of project management veterans interviewed for this book believe that most project managers who are less than honest about project success are eventually found out, resulting in greater harm to the project, the team, and especially the project manager. Deceptive reporting is a rookie mistake.

As mentioned in chapters 14 Not Recognizing That Half of Managing is Selling and 15 Failing Testing by Passing on Testing, one of the most important aspects of reporting to management honestly is *managing expectation*, specifically those of the corporate executives, business managers, end users, and IT. The best way to manage expectation is through frequent formal and informal meetings. Effective meetings require good *communication* skills that allow the project manager to tell the project's story, meaningfully and honestly, without getting bogged down in IT jargon or pie-chart purgatory.

Action

Facts are useless if they do not affect behavior and, in most cases, the sooner the better.

You need to ask yourself, why are there project managers? Why would an organization pay a lot of money to have someone who produces so little deliverable work? Is the project manager the most technical person on the team? Rarely. Overly technical people can be distracted by the technology and shortchange their managerial duties. No, a manager is paid the big bucks for doing two things: making the right decisions and acting on them.

Making the right decisions requires the two skills discussed above, *questioning* and *honesty*. To complete the trifecta, the manager then has to *act* on that decision. This is when the fan gets all messed up because the action might require changes to project plans that involve IT and/or user management. No one wants to stand before the corporate big dogs and say, oops, it's going to cost more than planned or take longer to deliver. However, if those are the facts, then the sooner the message is delivered and the necessary actions taken, the less those changes will cost and the more time the team will have to fix what has to be fixed.

Credibility

The trifecta—a combination of *questioning*, *honesty*, and *acting*—leads to *credibility*. It is the one thing that will convince user management to invest their staff, their money, and their future in you.

You know that credibility is at work when the project manager tells users they have nothing to worry about and the user community believes what the project manager is telling them because they have faith in the team, the process, and, most important, the project manager.

Trust

Take *credibility*, and its entourage of *questioning*, *honesty*, and *acting*, stir in a little time to ensure that these qualities are there for the long-run, and you arrive at *trust*, the holy grail of project management. Corporate executives, business managers, and users might have no idea what you do—in fact that is the point. Because they have no idea what you or the team does, they need to feel that you are competent, honest, and working in their best interest. If the goal posts need to move and the project will cost more, take longer, or not be able to deliver everything promised, then they need to feel that you did your best. Without *trust* every bit of bad news simply fulfills every stereotype they have held or heard about IT, and none of us want that.

Realization

By now, the reader should come to an important conclusion—communication is all important. Figure 18.1 shows that the project manager sits in the center of a web of communication. All recognize that the project manager needs to manage down to team members, both IT and user staff, who are aligning their corporate futures with the project and the project manager. However, to be successful, the project manager also needs to effectively manage up (even if that must be done through others) to senior executives who are concerned about placing the fate of the company in the hands of IT people. User management expands that concern to include the resources in dollars and staff they must commit to the project. Lastly, IT, so often the butt of cost and schedule overrun jokes, is concerned because it is placing its credibility in the hands of the project team and its manager.

As you read the above paragraphs, two things should become very clear. The first is that the project managers' knowledge of technology does not play the major role in project management. In fact, spending too much time on technical issues can consume the attention that project managers need to devote to other more important subjects. The second observation, and one of these "other more important subjects," is that communication is how project managers should spend the most significant portion of their time. Communicating important details to team members, or crafting summaries to senior executives, is time consuming if done right.

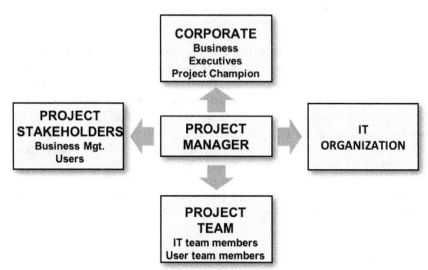

Figure 18.1 Project Management Communications Web

Most project manages have technical backgrounds. They were programmers or analysts who were promoted to project manager because they were good programmers or analysts and rarely because they had any proven project management skills. Many ill-prepared project managers fill the management-skill vacuum with their technical knowledge. However, if this book has done nothing else, it should convince you that project managers need a different skill set than the one that made them successful programmers or analysts.

Here is the consequential *realization* you will almost never hear from your boss, your mentor, your peers, or even from HR. **Moving from a technical role to a project management role is a career change.** Those who recognize the change can gain the needed skills and have a good chance of a successful career. Those who do not recognize that moving from technologist to manager is a career change will probably not learn the needed skills and are, sooner or later, doomed to failure.

AFTERWORD

Afterword

We dare not lengthen this book much more,
lest it be out of moderation and excite men's aversion through its magnitude.
~ Aelfric, Abbot of Eynsham (c. 955 – c. 1010)

To the Reader,

This book was a group effort. Many project managers, some know-ingly and many more unknowingly, contributed to this book, one way or another, although the final selection of the 17 problems and solutions was entirely mine. Let me explain.

I spent four decades of my life working on system development projects. Some projects were small 5- or 6-month efforts with a team of four or five developers while others were long (3 years and more) and large (more than 100 developers). I learned a great deal in those years—things every project manager should do as well as things that should be avoided. Like most project managers, I learned by doing, by watching, and especially by talking to project managers about their best and worst experiences.

The 17 problems in the book are an amalgamation of my experi-ences, the experiences of those I have worked with, and those I have interviewed, regarding the biggest problems facing the project manager along with practical, though not always widely recog-nized, solutions.

This book contains the memories, and sometimes nightmares, of project managers recounting the things they wished they had known and followed at some earlier time in their project manage-ment careers.

Not all of the project managers interviewed agreed that all of the 17 problems and solutions in the book are the most critical. However, all were willing to share *their* best experience and warn others with *their* worst horror story. I picked the problems and solutions I thought were the most common errors, had the greatest chance of early detection, and could be sufficiently corrected or mitigated if appropriate and timely action was taken.

I would be interested in hearing from readers like you about your project-related experiences—the good, the bad, and the ugly. I would like to know how problems were detected, the analysis used to uncover a solution, the decision process (who was involved and how they participated), and how the solution was acted upon. You can send your stories to me at my email address below. Who knows...maybe there will be another volume of project management problems and solutions sometime in the future with your experience used to educate the next generation of project managers.

If you like this book, write a review and either send it to me or post it online, such as on Amazon or Google.

You might also be interested in some of my other IT books.

Usage-Driven Database Design, Published by Apress, a division of Springer Nature.

The Business-Oriented CIO, Published by John Wiley & Sons.

A Practical Guide to Logical Data Modeling, Published by McGraw-Hill.

Best,
George Tillmann
george_tillmann@gmx.com
georgetillmann@optonline.net

APPENDIX

Appendix

Post-Project Review
Recalculating Project Effort
and
Creating a Reality Factor

As mentioned in Chapter 5 Planning for the Perfect, there is no easy and accurate way to estimate project effort that completely abrogates the *estimation conundrum* or *planning for the perfect*. This conundrum is the realization that when one estimates the effort to complete a task or system, in the estimator's mind is the picture of how the project will unfold *if* everything goes perfectly. Unfortunately, rarely does everything go perfectly, leading to thousands of underestimated projects.

Currently, there is no effective and accurate way to get around the problem, leaving the field open to mildly effective and partially accurate solutions. Here is one. The *Imperfect Method for Planning* (IMP) is a superficial and half-baked approach to minimizing the damage caused by *planning for the perfect*. It does this by uncritically defining a more *realistic estimate* (RE) as the perfect or *ideal estimate* (IE) plus an effort adjustment generated by a *reality factor* (RF).

A simple definition of the *Imperfect Method for Planning* would be a tongue-in-cheek recognition that a *realistic estimate* for any project is: (1) the *ideal estimate*, which assumes that every project task will complete without problems, on time, and on budget, plus (2) an effort adjustment calculated using an historical *reality factor*, which is the percent the *ideal estimate* needs to be modified to deliver a system that includes unanticipated interruptions, obstacles, and any other unplanned events. RE=IE+(IE*RF).

IMP relies on three concepts—

Ideal estimate (IE). The effort required to build a system if everything goes according to plan with no unanticipated events, interruptions, or obstacles.

Reality factor (RF). The project manager's personal or IT's organizational system development historical variance from the *ideal estimate*, expressed as a percent. The *reality factor* is used to determine the additional effort that needs to be added to the *ideal estimate* to create a *realistic estimate*.

Realistic estimate (RE). The *ideal estimate* plus an added adjustment, generated using the *reality factor*, to make the original *ideal estimate* more historically realistic.

Does calculating a project manager's personal or IT's organizational *reality factor* seem daunting? Here is a fairly simple way to accomplish it by reviewing one or more past projects.

Step 1. For each completed project task (where task is the generic term used for a project unit of work, such as a use case, story, etc.), determine, as accurately as possible, from documentation, the memory of the project manager, team members, etc., the *actual* effort required to complete each task. Call this the *actual task effort*.

Step 2. For each completed project task where 100 percent of the planned functionality *was* delivered to the user, total all of the individual a*ctual task effort*s giving the result *total actual task effort*.

Step 3. For each completed project task where 100 percent of the planned functionality was *not* delivered to the user:
(1) Estimate the percent of the planned functionality that *was* actually delivered, call it the *percent of work actually delivered*.
(2) Take the *actual task effort* created in Step 1 and add to it the effort that would be required to deliver the functionality that was *not* delivered. Call the result the *adjusted task effort*.
(3) Total all of the individual *adjusted task efforts* giving the result *total adjusted task effort*.

For example, if *actual task effort* for the task required 10 person-weeks and the *percent of work actually delivered* was 70%, then divide 10 (the effort) by 70% (the *percent of work actually delivered*) and you get the *adjusted task effort* of 14.3 person-weeks.

Step 4. Add together the *total actual task effort* and the *total adjusted task effort*. The result is the *realistic estimate* RE. The RE is the total effort that would have been required if all functionality was delivered.

Step 5. The difference between the *ideal estimate* IE (the total effort estimate in the project plan) and the RE is the project effort variance. The percent difference between the two is the project *reality factor* RF. For example, if the IE is 100 person-months and the RE is 120 person months then the RF is (120-100)/100 or 20 percent. RF=(RE-IE)/IE.

The project *reality factor* is one data point for the project manager's and/or IT's historical discrepancy between ideal (the perfect) and realistic project estimates.

In the future, a project *realistic estimate* can be created using the perfect *ideal estimate* and the *reality factor* using the formula RE=IE+(IE*RF).

For example, Figure A.1 Sample Completed Project is for a project with six planned tasks that require an estimated 74 person-months of effort. Three of the six tasks did not deliver all planned functionality. Adjusting for the missing functionality, the original estimate should have been 90.3 person months, a 22% increase over the original plan.

The 22% *reality factor* is a start for either the project manager and/or IT in generating a history-based *reality factor* for planning future development projects.

Will using the *reality factor* generate the correct amount of effort needed to build the next system? No. However, using it to generate a *realistic estimate* will result in a number closer to the actual effort spent than the *ideal estimate* and, over time, the *reality factor*—as its use expands and post-project data accumulates—will generate *realistic estimates* closer and closer to actual project effort.

Task	From Plan Ideal Estimate	Step 1 Actual Task Effort	Percent Functionality Delivered	Step 2 Total Actual Task Effort	Step 3 Total Adjusted Task Effort	Step 4 Realistic Estimate	Step 5 Reality Factor
1	10	11	100%	11			
2	6	8	100%	8			
3	15	14	100%	14			
4	8	9	70%		12.9		
5	21	24	80%		30.0		
6	14	13	90%		14.4		
Ideal Estimate (IE) 74							
Actual Project Effort		79					
Total Actual Task Effort				33			
Total Adjusted Task Effort					57.3		
Realistic Estimate (RE)						90.3	
Reality Factor (RF)							22%

Figure A.1 Sample Completed Project

GLOSSARY

Glossary

Actual What really happened. For example, in systems development there are three significant actuals: *cost*, *effort*, and *time*.

Agile development An iterative and incremental development approach that stresses collaborative continual improvement using a number of modern development techniques.

Bell curve See Normal distribution.

Budget The *costs* (*funds*) and *schedule* (*time*) granted or allocated to a project to complete its work. Occasionally used to refer to the funds only.

Change control A formal project management process that documents user and IT requests for a change to an ongoing project, assesses the impact of the change, provides both benefits and costs, rates them on a formal scale, and presents them to a change control committee for disposition. The committee will then decide whether the change is warranted and should be made now; is unwarranted and should be rejected; or warranted but should be not be implemented until a future time.

Client A customer who has an ongoing relationship with a business or vendor.

Communication overhead The resources required for team members to keep each other apprised of project activities. As the headcount of the team increases, the communication overhead rises exponentially.

Conceptual definition An intangible, theoretical, and abstract concept that you hold to be true.

Constructive cost model (COCOMO) A formula-based systems development cost model developed by Barry Boehm.

Consumer A customer who has a transactional relationship with a business or vendor.

Cost The funds (money for hardware, software, personnel, occupancy, etc.) allocated or required to complete the project.

Customer Anyone who buys or acquires a product or service from a business or vendor. (See Client, Consumer.)

Definitional problem The unforeseen consequences that result from multiple parties unknowingly having multiple well-defined definitions, or using multiple but not all well-defined definitions, or using non-specific, fuzzy, or incomplete definitions.

Deliverable desert The time between project kickoff and the first user deliverable and between subsequent user deliverables.

Delphi method An example of an expert-based estimating technique.

Dream time The time between receipt of user-articulated requirements and a delivery of a system supporting those requirements. The longer the dream time the greater the chance users will "dream up" new or different requirements.

Effort The amount of work needed or applied to complete a task. In systems development, effort is most commonly expressed in person-years, person-months, person-weeks, person-days, or person-hours, where a person-month is the amount of work one person can produce in 1 month.

Estimate An approximation of a calculable value. In systems development, there are three significant estimates: *cost*, *effort*, and *time*.

Estimation conundrum The tongue-in-cheek awareness that no matter what a project manager does, he or she is destined to underestimate the effort required for a project.

Experimental-based estimating Estimating approaches that involve the developer performing a small amount of actual work on the project and then stopping, measuring progress, and then, using that data, projecting the effort needed to complete the entire project.

Expert-based estimating (also called a guru-based estimating) A project estimating technique that gathers systems development and business experts together and, through interviews, surveys, and/or group meetings, arrives at a group educated guess of the effort required to complete a project. Delphi is an example of an expert-based technique.

Forecast A projection or prediction of a future event or state.

Formula-based estimating Estimating approaches that center on the project manager answering a number of questions that are then entered into a model. The model, a calculator- or computer-based program, then calculates the effort needed. SLIM (Software Lifecycle Management), developed by Lawrence Putnam; COCOMO (Constructive Cost Model), developed by Barry Boehm; and Function Point Analysis, originally conceived by Allan Albrecht; are examples of formula-based estimating techniques.

Fudge factor An arbitrary number applied to an estimate to increase its chances of being correct or accepted.

Full-time equivalent (FTE) (1) the ratio of the actual hours a team member works compared with hours defined as full-time. (2) a virtual team member.

Function point analysis A formula-based systems development cost model originally conceived by Allan Albrecht.

Functionality What the system does or is supposed to do.

Fundamental principle of systems development (FPSD) The principle that espouses figuring out *what* the system is supposed to do before determining *how* to do it.

Funds See Cost.

Fungible An asset that can be substituted for another asset of the same kind. Fungible objects have no individuation and are interchangeable with all other objects of the same class.

Gaussian distribution See Normal distribution.

Guru-based estimating See Expert-based estimating.

History-based estimating Estimating approaches that look into the organization's past to predict the effort required for similar completed projects. SLIM (Software Lifecycle Management), developed by Lawrence Putnam, is an example of a history-based technique.

Honeymoon period The short period of time between project kickoff and when the project becomes fair game for project naysayers.

Housekeeping phase See Infrastructure phase.

How In systems development, the approach, design, and execution required to realize the *what* (*what* the system should do). The *how* creates and delivers to the user *what* the user requested.

Ideal estimate (IE) In the *Imperfect Method for Planning (IMP)* approach, the effort required to build a system if everything goes as planned.

Imperfect method for planning (IMP) A tongue-in-cheek recognition that a *realistic estimate (RE)* for any project is the *ideal estimate* (IE), which assumes that every project task will complete without problems, on time, and on budget; plus an historically calculated *reality factor* (RF), which is the average additional work required to deliver a system owing to unanticipated interruptions, obstacles, and any other unplanned events. It is expressed by the formula RE=IE+RF.

Infrastructure phase The part of a project that involves creating the technical environment, such as the hardware, networks, system software, and development tools, necessary to developed a system.

Iterative and/or incremental (I-I) systems development approaches The name for multiple SDLCs, that reject the waterfall approach by making systems development a series of small iterative and/or incremental steps, each of which identifies a small portion of the overall application and creates an equally small portion of the deliverable.

Managing expectation The near continual, honest, and unvarnished feedback to the user about what the system is supposed to do (its functionality), progress IT has made in building the system (realizing that functionality), and what IT and the user need to do to successfully complete the project.

Method A detailed systems development approach or SDLC for applying one or more techniques that usually includes the sequence of steps to be performed, deliverables to be produced, discipline to be followed, and project management steps to be executed.

Methodology See Method.

Negative variance When *actuals* exceed *planed*. An unfavorable variance.

Mid-project blues A period of anxiety caused by the deliverable desert.

Normal distribution A graph depicting a curve whose distribution, dispersion, or variation of data on the left side of the curve mirrors that on the right side of the curve.

Operational definition A limited and sometimes temporary agreement to use a precise definition in a specific context.

Person-month The amount (unit) of work one person can complete in 1 calendar month. For example, two person-months is the amount of work one person can complete in 2 months or two people in 1 month.

Planning for the perfect The realization that when one estimates the effort to complete a task or system, in the estimator's mind is the picture of how the effort will unfold if everything goes perfectly.

Perfectam consilium See Planning for the perfect.

Positive variance When *planned* exceeds *actuals*. A favorable variance.

Productivity The amount of quality work completed by a team member or team in a unit of time.

Project champion. A senior member of the organization who takes a personal interest in the project. The champion can speak for the organization at project meetings and reviews and has the power to influence, if not modify, budgets and project plans, and commit organizational resources.

Project evaluation and review technique (PERT) An estimating technique that requires three estimates: *optimistic, pessimistic,* and *most likely,* representing the minimum possible time, the best estimate, and the maximum possible time required, respectively, to complete the project.

Project glossary A formal list of the terms and definitions created to describe, explain, and communicate to senior, business unit, and IT management and to user and IT staff the concepts, deliverables, and language used during the project.

Project management review survival techniques Four rules to follow when presenting to management. (1) A good presentation presents a story that the audience can take with them when they leave. (2) Every problem should be accompanied by a well thought out solution. (3) Focus on the future (when will the project finish, what will it cost, what will the system do?). (4) Always pre-sell bad news to the project champion and/or one or two senior managers before the meeting. No Surprises.

Project plan A formal document that serves as an agreement between IT and the user to guide the development of a computer-based application. The plan includes a description (in varying levels of detail) of the system to be built (the scope), the development requirements (hardware, software, staff (both IT and user), etc.) to build the system, the responsibilities of all parties, schedules, and all costs (as detailed as possible). A good plan also includes an agreement on an adjudication process for resolving discrepancies and disagreements, a change control process for mid-project requests for modifications to the system or project plan, a process for defining when testing and other systems development components are complete, and a post-project review process to assess what went according to plan and what did not.

Project sweet spot The hypothetical ideal project team size of between four and seven staff and 3 to 9 months duration. It is a fictitious project size created for this book from an examination of numerous studies of team size productivity.

Quality (software) Computer code that meets or exceeds standards of form and structure, meets or exceeds all functional (user) requirements, contains no serious errors, is well documented, and is easily understandable by other experienced coders.

Rapid-application development (RAD) Any of a series of methods or techniques to speed up the development of software by stressing the use of tools, prototyping, iterative, or incremental development.

Rapid Systems Development See Rapid-application development.

Realistic estimate (RE) In the *Imperfect Method for Planning (IMP)* approach, the *ideal estimate* plus an added adjustment, generated using the *reality factor*, to make the original *ideal estimate* more historically realistic.

Reality factor (RF) In the *Imperfect Method for Planning (IMP)* approach, the historical project manager's personal or IT's organizational systems development variance from the *idea estimate* expressed as a percent. The *reality factor* is used to determine the additional effort that needs to be added to the *ideal estimate* to create a *realistic estimate*.

Schedule Also referred to as *time*, is the calendar months (weeks, days, etc.) required to complete a project.

Scope creep The tendency of the user community to slowly add features to a system during development often without sufficient regard for their consequences.

Scope Technically the specification of the extent and breadth of the system (functionality, number/type of users, performance, location or geography covered, times of operation) to determine exactly what is in and what is out of the system. However, it is most commonly used to mean simply functionality—which features are part of the system and which are not.

SDLC See Systems development life cycle.

Seed A starting point for an estimating technique. In most cases a number varying from randomly selected to an educated guess to kick-off an estimating process.

Senior management The most senior executives in an organization.

Slippage The usually gradual failure to meet a planned deadline, milestone, checkpoint, or target.

Software lifecycle management (SLIM) A history-based cost model developed by Lawrence Putnam.

Stakeholder An individual who holds a vested interest in a business or project. For a system development projects, stakeholders are senior and business unit management but can also include users, IT management, and IT staff.

Story A unit of work in agile development akin to a use case in object development or a task in traditional approaches.

Systems development life cycle (SDLC) A formal process for the planning, analyzing, designing, developing, testing, and implementing a computer-based system.

Task A defined piece of work performed by a team in an allotted period of time to produce a defined deliverable.

Technique A series of steps applied to a subject to change its representation. Data modeling, processing modeling, and prototyping are all techniques.

Three planning variables Cost, time, and functionality.

Three ultimate questions The three most important questions stakeholders (senior and business unit management), IT management, and users want answered. (1) Is the project on schedule?—Will the project end when is supposed to end? (2) Is the project on budget?—Will the project cost what it was projected to cost? (3) Will it work? Will the system do what it was promised to do—features and quality?

Throwaway code The temporary software programs and routines created to help in the coding, testing, conversion, and implementation of the final (deliverable) system.

Time See Schedule.

Tool A physical or conceptual product that aids in applying techniques. CASE products and flow-charting templates are tools.

Top three/bottom three survival technique The three major positive answers and the three major issues or concerns to each of the *Three Ultimate Questions*.

Underestimation gene A tongue-in-cheek explanation of why humans so often underestimate effort.

Use Case An analysis technique, usually associated with an object-oriented system development approach, for identifying and describing in detail a discrete unit of work to accomplish a particular task between a user and the system.

Users Those who commission the building of an information system, represent those who commission the system, or will use the system commissioned. They are usually non-technical staff (unless the system is designed to serve technical staff, e.g., an application tracking system).

Variance The difference between *forecast* and *actual*. A *positive variance* results when planned exceeds actuals. A *negative variance* results when actuals exceed planned. For example, a *positive cost variance* occurs when less funds are expended than planned.

Waterfall approach See Waterfall systems development life cycle.

Waterfall method See Waterfall systems development life cycle.

Waterfall systems development life cycle The development of a system using a series of sequential steps and phases Each phase is executed only once at the completion of the previous phase. A simple waterfall approach might consist of five phases such as analysis, design, coding, testing, and implementation.

What In systems development, the formal or informal specification of the functionality the user wants the system to perform. The name is derived for expressions such as: *what* is needed, *what* the user wants, *what* the system should do. The *what* is commonly associated with the request for proposal and system requirements phases.

Work breakdown structure (WBS) A hierarchical project organizational approach that divides a project into manageable *tasks*. Each task is assigned to a team to produce a defined deliverable in an allotted period of time.

Working definition See Operational definition.

INDEX

Index

www.ingramcontent.com/pod-product-compliance
Lightning Source LLC
Chambersburg PA
CBHW071115050326
40690CB00008B/1233